THE SACRAMENTAL SOCIETY

THE SACRAMENTAL SOCIETY

By C. RYDER SMITH,

B.A., D.D. (Lond.)

Tutor in Theology, Richmond College, Surrey

Published for the
FERNLEY LECTURE TRUST

LONDON

THE EPWORTH PRESS

J. ALFRED SHARP

First Edition July, 1927

Made and Printed in Great Britain by
The Camelot Press Limited,
London and Southampton

TO EVERY READER WHO DISAGREES
WITH ME

CONTENTS

CONTENTS

The Sacramental Society

I

THE SUBJECT AND METHOD OF THE LECTURE

OF the controversies that have divided the Church of Christ one is peculiarly active to-day. It is the controversy about the Church, the Ministry, and the Sacraments. Of other controversies some seem dead and some asleep, but this one is alive and wakeful. For more than three hundred years it has distracted a large part of Christendom. It still sets one church against another, or one party against another within the same church. Hitherto it has intractably thwarted the enterprise of Christian Reunion. In spite of its many difficulties, however—or, rather, because of them—it still challenges the careful and charitable consideration of Christian men. We cannot just leave it where it is.

The controversy has many parts, but perhaps they all fall under two principles. These are the principle of authority, and what I may briefly call the Sacramental principle. The two are closely related—so closely as often to intertwine—yet they are distinguishable. It is with the second that we have here to do.

The leading questions of this part of the controversy may be briefly stated. To the vast majority of Christians, by whatever name they are called, the two Sacraments of Baptism and the Lord's Supper are a very precious possession. They all believe that in the Sacraments there is something belonging to the material world and something belonging to the spiritual world. In Baptism the material thing is water, in the Lord's Supper the material things are bread and wine. While it is not so easy to find an agreed name for the spiritual element, all claim that there is something spiritual in the two Sacraments. Disagreement begins when *the relation between* the material and the spiritual is examined.[1]

Again, a large majority of Christians set apart their Ministers by the ' laying on of hands ' or Ordination. Here too there is something that belongs to the material world, and something that belongs to the spiritual. All, of course, admit that the act of Ordination itself is of an outward, visible, and material kind, while all claim that unless something spiritual goes with it, it is naught. Yet when an attempt is made to define the relation between the two, controversy begins. Another instance of the mystery of the relation between the inward and the outward emerges. It is plain that the same is true of other related subjects, as, for instance, of Confirmation. The problem of the relation between the outward and inward, the physical and psychological, the material and spiritual, recurs.

No attempt is made here to cover the whole ground of the controversy in question. It has been treated in various ways. Appeal, for instance, has often been made to Christian history. The regulative question in this method is : What has been the custom of the Church ? Many who have pursued this question have asserted, argued, or assumed, that the custom of the Church in the past is of final authority for the Church now. I do not hold this opinion, and perhaps few hold it in its absolute form, for this would mean that the Church has

---

[1] Some writers, when treating of the Real Presence, use the term ' spiritual ' to include the physical. This does not seem to me a happy use, nor do I think that it is rightly grounded in Paul.

no right ever to change anything. All Christians claim
that the Church is still under the guidance of the Holy
Spirit, and that to-day, as in every past day, He shows to
those who ' will receive it ' the right way to deal with the
perennial novelty of life. This means that there will be
change. The differences between Christians are really
about the *extent* of change, or, to put the same truth in
another way, about the degree and extent of authorita-
tiveness that belong to the custom and rule of the Church
in the past. There is a place for this historical method
of investigation, and for the discussion of the nature
of authority that attends it, but this is not the method
followed here. [1]

Another method of investigation may be called the
biblical. Its normative question is : What is the teaching
of the Bible, and particularly of the New Testament ?
It is possible, of course, to define this investigation as
but part of the historical, for the New Testament tells
the story of the earliest period of Church History, and
the Old Testament is its historical prelude and preparation. Yet it is convenient to treat the biblical method
as distinct from the historical, for many Christians admit
an authority in the Apostles that they would not allow
in any later leaders of the Church, and all Christians claim
that the authority of our Lord Himself is unique and
supreme. This method of investigation, too, therefore,
is both legitimate and valuable, but it is not the one
primarily followed here. For while there are whole
chapters below that discuss the passages in the New Testament that are pertinent to the subject, they occur in the
course of the pursuit of another method.

What is this method ? It has not been followed

---

[1] There are indeed incidental references to history, and two passages deal
at some length with certain historical phenomena (chap ii., *D*, and chap. iii.),
but in both cases the historical is subordinate and illustrative, not regulative.
I have discussed the nature of authority on two of its sides in *The Bibl*
Doctrine of Society, chap. vi., and *The Christian Experience*, chap. xx.

nearly as often as the historical or the biblical, and it is not very easy to give it a name. Perhaps it might be called the ' psychological,' or the ' analogical.' It treats the theological problem as an example of a wider problem, and asks what light is thereby shed upon it.

This wider problem may be put under the question, ' How are the spiritual and the material worlds related to each other ? ' Two illustrative instances may be named. What is the relation between the spiritual and the material, the soul and the body, in man ? This is the most obvious instance of the problem, and shows at once how baffling it is. For we know that the soul and body are one, but, even after millenniums of thought, we have no inkling how they are one. To use a technical term, the two are as disparate as two things can be— that is, they belong to quite different realms of existence— yet the two are one. It is true that current thought, reversing the hypothesis of materialism, begins to suggest that the body may be the product of the soul, or, in broader phrase, that matter may be the product of mind. But this does not really bridge the gulf that lies between them. How does mind ' produce ' matter ? What is meant by ' production '? No one knows. There are some, indeed, who seem to think that, if the physicist reduces matter to motion, he has thereby made it more like mind, but a moment's reflection shows that this is not so. In practice we every moment cross the gulf between mind and matter, soul and body, with the ease of a bird, but as yet no one has even begun to explain the easy feat.

A second instance of the problem of the relation of the spiritual and the material worlds falls under the question, ' What is the relation of God, who is pure Spirit, to the universe ? ' The usual Christian answer is summed under the two terms ' transcendence ' (or, in older phraseology, ' creation,') and ' immanence,' but perhaps no terms have covered greater ignorance. Neither idea has ever been adequately explored, as all philosophers tell us. Other examples might be added. The mystery of the relation between the spiritual world and the material is both pervasive and baffling. Under the subjects of the Ministry and the Sacraments it intrudes, in yet another way, on Christian thought.

An obvious question ensues. If the wider problem be unresolved, if it be properly named a mystery, how can its study help any one to understand one of its particular instances? The answer is that while the subject of the relation of the spiritual and material, the outward and inward, is a mystery, yet there are some things that can be asserted about it. Some results are obtainable. Some laws can be observed. The suggestion here made is that what is true in the realm of the wider problem is likely to be true also in the realm of our particular instance. In other words, the argument is by analogy. The next chapters will show more clearly what is meant. I do not wish, however, to hide the fact that there is here an assumption. It is assumed that between the problem as it occurs in life at large and the problem as it occurs in the Church, there are likenesses. Some will deny this altogether, and affirm that the doctrine of the Sacraments, for instance, has no parallels. They claim that in every Sacrament there is ' miracle.' This subject, as I think, is best discussed after the argument that I wish to urge has been laid out. It is examined, therefore, in an appendix. [1]

Again, others may urge that, while there are likenesses between the instances of the spiritual-material relation that occur in general human experience and those that belong specially to the Church, there will also be differences. In logical terminology, they will claim that the latter have their own *differentiae*. This is true. Some attempt is therefore made below to define the distinctive characteristics of the relation of the outward and inward

[1] p. 213.

in its Christian instances.   The broad order of the
discussion is as follows : First, the argument from
analogy is drawn out, the Christian use of symbols being
both compared and contrasted with other uses.   This
fills the next chapter ; in it the subject of Ordination is
discussed.   In the third chapter there is an historical
survey of the teaching of the Bible on the general subject
of the relation between the inward and outward in the
religious life.   It may serve, not only to illustrate the
contentions of the second chapter, but to show that the
differences of opinion on the subject under discussion are
practically important.   It is desirable that this be done,
for the ' lay mind,' as some call it, is prone to cry out upon
the exact discussions of students as the ' hair-splitting of
trifles.'   The fourth and fifth chapters discuss the Sacraments of Baptism and the Lord's Supper.   The last
chapter examines the bearing of the conclusions reached
on the subjects of Church-membership, Inter-Communion,
and Christian Reunion.

It may be that some, as they read later chapters, will
think that I too often use the phrases ' It seems to me,'
and ' This subject cannot be fully discussed here ' !   The
use of the first phrase is to be explained by the
eirenic temper of which mention is made below.   The
second cannot be avoided in a lecture on such a subject.
If all the questions involved in a discussion of the Sacramental principle were examined, large volumes would be
needed on psychology, philosophy, and theology.   It is
one of the curious marks of our time that people make
two demands of writers—that every book shall be short,
yet that it shall discuss everything !   Happily some
allowance is still made to lecturers, as distinct from other
writers—a lecturer is only expected to deal with one phase
of his subject. [1]

---

[1] Only a part of the Lecture, of course, was delivered, but I have used the
form of a lecture, rather than a book, throughout.

Of the questions that ' cannot be fully discussed here '
I ought to make special mention of two.   The first is,
' Did our Lord Himself institute or authorize the Sacraments of Baptism and the Lord's Supper, and did He
mean them to be perpetual in His Church ? '   The second
is, ' How far did the Mystery Religions influence the
Apostolic Church ? '   My answers to both are of a
conservative type—yet the answers may still be true.
I believe that our Lord authorized the use of the Sacrament of Baptism and instituted the Sacrament of the
Lord's Supper, and that He meant both to be perpetual in
His Church.   I do not believe that the two Sacraments
were interpreted in Apostolic times after the manner of
the Mystery Religions.   Something is said on these
subjects incidentally below, and something is added in
the Appendix, but neither is fully discussed.

Another remark may be added about method.   The
subject of the Lecture is, of course, controversial, but it
need not therefore be pursued as a polemic.   Polemics
may sometimes be justifiable, but they are not usually
fruitful.   One of the marks of Christian thought to-day is
its eirenic temper.   We are not so set as our fathers were
upon disputatious victories.   We all yearn to be one, and
the reunion of Christendom haunts many minds.   In
consequence controversial subjects are approached in a
new spirit.   Men in opposite camps want to understand
one another and, if possible, to win one another.   They
are ready to make any sacrifice short of the sacrifice of
truth—or, as many of them would more carefully say, of
what appears to them to be truth.   Not a few books,
therefore, that deal with the subjects of the Church, the
Ministry, and the Sacraments, seek chiefly to set out as
clearly as possible the opinions of their writers and to give
the grounds of those opinions, rather than to overthrow
the arguments of opponents.   This is the method followed
here.   As far as may be, the polemic attitude has been

avoided, and the explanatory attitude adopted. I hope against hope that this brief statement of what I take to be true Sacramentalism, may be of some small service in the great and slow task of the reunion of Christendom.

I need to add two brief remarks of a personal kind. Not infrequently, where there are allusions to subjects that are not fully discussed, I have ventured to refer to previous books of mine, expecially to the volume entitled *The Christian Experience*. And I am indebted to four friends for reading the book, either in typescript or in proof, and making a number of valuable suggestions—my wife, and my colleagues, Rev. Dr. H. Maldwyn Hughes, Rev. Dr. Eric S. Waterhouse, and Rev. F. Bertram Clogg, M.A., B.D.

II

THE SYMBOLIC AND THE SACRAMENTAL

A. SOCIETIES, PERSONS, AND THINGS

IT will be convenient to examine some of the general
phenomena of the relation of the spiritual to the material
world, before asking how far they obtain in the particular
instances presented by the Church. When the general
subject is examined, a great distinction at once emerges.
There are two kinds of spiritual ' realities ' or ' entities,'
individual persons and societies, and their relations to the
material world agree in some ways but differ in others.

It is said that when Dr. Parker was asked, ' Has man a
soul ? ' he replied, ' Man *is* a soul, and *has* a body.'
Some psychologists would disagree and prefer to say that
man is body-soul. But all would assert that the fundamental relation of the ' spirit ' of individual men to the
world of ' matter ' is through the body. Further, Christian
thinkers would be unanimous in rejecting the tenet of
materialism that the ' spirit ' or ' soul ' is a product of the
body, and would claim that, in the unity that may be
called ' body-soul,' it is the soul that is the more
important. They would not say, ' The body has a soul,'
but they would either say, ' The soul has a body,' or ' In
the unity of soul and body, it is the soul that is and ought
to be the dominant partner ; it is the body's business to
serve it.' And when at death the two part company,
Christian thinkers agree that the ' personality ' belongs
to the soul and not to the body. At the same time they

B

do not despise the body, but agree that, at least in this life, the body is integral to human personality.

Has a *society* a body? Has it a soul? Or is it a soul-body? Philosophers and psychologists differ greatly in their definitions of a ' society,' and it may be that, when their differences disappear in more nearly certain knowledge, unexpected light will fall upon some of the problems of the Church, but, apart again from sheer materialists, psychologists agree that societies are spiritual. It is significant, however, that they do not generally use the term ' soul ' about societies, though they may speak of their common ' spirit,' a distinction which the ' man in the street ' also makes in his speech. Why is this? The reason appears to be that of the two synonyms, ' soul ' and ' spirit,' the first denotes the spiritual in man considered as connected with a body, while the second denotes the spiritual in man without this connexion. In other words, psychology and ' common sense ' agree that societies have not bodies. They are not physical, as individuals are. Here is an important difference between the two kinds of spiritual entities.

But how is it then that societies are so often called bodies? What do we mean by such phrases as ' body politic '? Why do we naturally call a University or a school a ' body '? Why do we freely apply the adjective ' corporate ' and the noun ' corporation ' to societies? Why do people who cannot honestly use the word ' church ' of Nonconformists, fall back upon the term ' body '?

The answer is that the use is metaphorical. To some this may seem obvious, but it has often been forgotten or overlooked, with confusing consequences. For a metaphor, of course, involves a comparison of two things, and two things are never altogether alike, and to use a metaphor where it does not apply is a frequent source of error. When a society is called a body, and the people

who belong to it are called its ' members,' it is not meant
that the society is a physical entity and has a body, but
that it is a unity, and a unity of the living type—in other
words, that it is organic.   Yet even the last word may
mislead, for it suggests ' organism ' and ' organization,'
and these suggest the material world, the second of
them even the mechanical world.   But a society has an
organism that is spiritual.   It is a living and inter-related
whole, even though it is not physical.   And the terms
' body ' and ' corporate ' are good metaphorical terms
for this kind of unity.   But they are not to be taken
literally.   Every one knows the story of the visitor to
Oxford who, after seeing many great sights, turned to
his guide and said, ' But you have not shown me the
University itself ; where is it ? '   A University may be
properly called a ' body,' or, if one prefers long phrases,
' an academic corporation,' but this does not mean that
it has a physical counterpart in the way in which the soul
of an individual person has a body.   It means that its
life is one, yet manifold—that its ' members ' share a
common, inter-related life, in which each serves and is
served by all the others—that it is spiritually organic, if
the phrase may be allowed.   In other words, the metaphor
' body ' is apt as suggesting organic life, but inapt as
suggesting physical counterpart.

The visitor to Oxford, however, had no doubt been
shown many colleges, and it may seem that here there
is an example of a society with a body, for the term
' college ' is applied both to a society and to the building
that is its habitat.   But a moment's thought shows that
the nearer parallel here is not with the individual's use
of his body, but with his use of other things.   A college-
building is to the society that inhabits it as a man's
house is to the man that lives in it, rather than as the
body is to the soul.   Common speech here again is correct.
We call a college-building the ' home ' of the society, not

its ' body.' This is clearer still if other examples of the
relation of societies to the material world be taken. A
society like the British nation may own armaments and
post offices and convicts' clothes, but these are its property or tools, not its body. The way in which societies
use ' things ' is rather like that in which individuals use
' the world outside ' than the way in which they use their
bodies in particular. Of course, here too there are
differences. An individual reaches these other things
through his body, while a society has no physical counterpart to serve such a turn. Instead it has to reach them
through one or more of the individual persons that are
its ' members.' In other words, a society, unlike an
individual, has no direct use of things at all. The direct
use of things is always individual. College-buildings are
directly used by individuals, not by the college itself, as
a spiritual entity, for it does not need a roof to shelter it
or a board to feed from or a bed to sleep on. Still,
societies do make an indirect use of the material world,
but the nearest parallel in the life of individuals is their
use of tools[1] and not their use of bodies.

A word should perhaps be said here about the
' aesthetic ' use of ' things.' It is claimed by many that a
true work of art is not wholly material. They say that
the artist has added something spiritual to the material
medium in which he works, and that it is this spiritual
something that makes a work of art. The vagueness of
the account of what this spiritual something is, does
not disprove this claim, for the study of the science of
aesthetics is still in its infancy. It is true, again, that the
Church has been prolific of works of art, as her many
masterpieces in architecture, painting, and music show.
This truth, however, has little bearing on the present
study, for the particular use of the material world made
in the Sacraments and in Ordination leaves small scope

[1] The word is here used in its wide sense, to include property

for aesthetic treatment, and no one has ever based their
value upon their beauty. Again, while all agree that
here pre-eminently ' all things should be done decently
and in order,' no one argues that Sacramental acts are
ipso facto invalid if they are not aesthetically performed.
The difficult questions of aesthetics may here, therefore,
be left on one side.

Yet societies do use the material world in a characteristic way. It is characteristic, even though it, too, is best
approached by way of an individual use. One of the chief
functions of spiritual beings is thought. Individuals
express the spiritual products called thoughts by material
means. The commonest instance is speech. Every
language consists of a multitude of ' words,' and a word is
a connected series of sounds. For instance, the English
have selected the two sounds ' fah ' and ' ther ' to denote
the idea ' male parent ' ; the Romans preferred the two
sounds ' pa ' and ' ter.' Sound, of course, belongs to the
material world, for it is produced by air-vibrations. The
way in which the vibrations turn into ideas is an
unfathomed mystery, yet sound is still material and
not spiritual. The next example is writing. Here the
appeal is not to the ear, but to the eye. Certain agreed
combinations of marks called letters, when gathered into
larger combinations called ' words,' are taken as tokens
of ideas. But, while speech and writing are the two
greatest instances of the use of things material as symbols
of things spiritual, they are not the only ones. Touches
may be used as symbols too, as in the nose-rubbing of the
South Sea Islander or the hand-shake and the kiss of the
European. Here there is a particular example of the way
in which individual spiritual beings use material things as
tools—they make them into symbols. And here is the
distinctive term—this use of the material world is
called ' symbolic.'

But, already, in describing this particular use of the

material world, we have passed insensibly from individuals to societies. The English language is the product of a great society, and the Latin of another. And, while no doubt individual people may sometimes use symbols merely as means of self-expression—as when a child shouts ' hurrah ' though he is alone—or as convenient memory helps—as when a man makes a note in his pocket-book—yet the chief use of symbols is not individual but societary. By their means the ' members ' of a given society communicate with each other. In other words, symbols are the universal media of fellowship. There is no need to stay to discuss the difficult question whether human beings ever communicate with each other without symbols—as appears to be the case in telepathy ; it is enough that in ordinary life communication always proceeds by symbols. So far as we can see, there could be no such thing as a human society at all without this material means of fellowship. If there were no symbols of a material kind—no speech, no writing, no printing, no symbolic touches even—there could not be such a thing as a nation, a church, a home. The symbolic use of the material world is the distinctively societary use. Here again the aesthetic intrudes. For it is by the artistic use and development of language that literature emerges. But here again no one makes the aesthetic use funda- mental or essential. Here again, too, while religion makes aesthetic use of symbols in such works of art as the great liturgies, it is not this use that is pertinent to the present inquiry. Societies are spiritual entities, but, unlike individual spiritual beings, they consist of parts that are themselves spiritual entities, and these find their means of fellowship in material symbols. Symbols are essential to societies.

The use of symbols will be more minutely examined directly, but perhaps this is the best place to advert to the phrase ' mere symbols.' It may even be that some

readers, having read the above paragraphs, are already
saying to themselves, ' Yes, his view is the merely
symbolic view.' May I point out, therefore, that, on the
account just given, the phrase ' mere symbol ' is a
contradiction in terms ? A symbol belongs indeed to the
material world, but, unless it has a spiritual correlative, it
is not a symbol, but has degenerated into a form. The
correct phrase is ' mere forms.' Symbols are among the
most important things in the life of man. This has
already been implied. Does any one say about a
literature or a kiss that it is ' merely symbolic ' ?
Symbol is as necessary to bind the universe of persons
together as gravity the world of things. No symbols,
no societies.

B. THE USE OF SYMBOLS

As the symbolic use of material things is the characteristic use when societies are being considered, it may be
well to look at it a little more closely. The common
symbols of fellowship, as the hand-shake or kiss, have
often been compared with the Sacramental uses of the
Church, but the comparison has not often been drawn
out. It seems to me worth while to draw it out, and to
begin by examining in greater detail the use of symbols
outside the Church.

As has already been seen, no society can exist without
symbols, for societies live by fellowship, and symbols are
the universal medium of fellowship. Probably the Friends
make as near an approach as any society to the discarding
of symbols. Yet of course they do not fully discard them,
nor claim to do so. As soon as any one speaks at all in a
' Quakers' Meeting,' he uses the symbols called words.
Once, when attending such a gathering, I noticed that two

of the older men gave the signal for the close of the meeting by shaking hands. I have learnt since that in older days such meetings broke up with a universal hand-shaking. The hand-shake is a symbol. A devout Friend once told me that in many Meetings it would be counted almost intolerable that any one should speak during the first quarter of an hour. Is there not here a kind of silent symbol? And if any rebelled against the custom, would not his first word, whatever it was, be a symbol of his rebellion? Other societies, of course, make no attempt even to reduce their use of symbols to a minimum. Some, as the Freemasons, seem almost to revel in their multiplication. Many societies, again, have their own peculiar symbols, as when a nation crowns its king or when the members of a University wear a gown. Multitudes of instances will occur to every reader. Symbols are essential to societies. They are the implements of their organic unity.

But there is a complementary truth—while no society can exist, still less flourish, without the use of symbols, no particular symbol is essential to any society. Probably the kind of symbol that is commonest, speech, comes nearest to being indispensable, but it seems certain that a society could exist without it. The deaf and dumb hold fellowship without its symbols, while even among other men writing is always an alternative to speaking, and often a more convenient one. Again, within the realm of speech and writing there is an almost endless choice of symbols, for the number of languages is legion, and, of course, every language is just one more set of symbols. The ring is an almost universal symbol of marriage in the ‘white world,’ but no one would to-day say that an old-fashioned Quaker, if he refuses that symbol, cannot marry, or claim that, among the millions of brown and yellow and black men, who do not use the symbol of the ring, there is no true marriage at all. The ex-Kaiser never went to Königsberg to be crowned, but he was still King of Prussia, as many another symbol showed. When James II, in flight from London, threw the Great Seal into the Thames, he was merely childish ; the Acts of the English Parliament could be made valid by a new seal or without one at all. Every society must use symbols, but no society is ' tied up ' to any particular symbol.

A distinction should be drawn here between the terms ' essential ' and ' obligatory.' The second term introduces the notion of authority. To discuss the nature of authority does not fall here, but I may state one or two of my convictions about it. It does not seem to me that the authority of a society is external to its members. This cannot be so, if they are really ' part and parcel ' of it.[1] Next, while there may be dispute about the limits of the authority of a society, all admit that within its *agreed* limits a society has the right to select its own symbols, and, when they are selected, it is obligatory on its members to observe them. The instance of the ring in marriage has been taken above. It is well known that the first Quakers refused to use that symbol, and that the State at last allowed that a marriage could be legal without it. But the question they raised was, Is the society called the State, to which we Quakers belong, exceeding its authority in selecting a symbol for marriage ? For those English people who agree that this selection is within the right of the State, the use of the ring is obligatory, though not essential, in marriage. Or again, while worship is essential in religion, the use of Sunday as the day of worship is not essential but obligatory. Or again, when people object to Summer Time on the ground that we ' cannot alter nature,' they are confusing the obligatory and the essential. Or again, a new society called the

---

[1] The chapter ' Authority and Fellowship ' in my volume *The Christian Experience* draws out this statement.

League of Nations has recently been born at Geneva. One of its first practical problems was to decide what language or languages should be used at its meetings— that is, by what sets of symbols its members should communicate with each other. It decided that, in whatever language a speech were delivered, it must be rendered into English and French. No one would maintain that either of these sets of symbols is essential to the League ; Spanish or Latin or Pushtu would serve. But all the members of the society agree that this is a point within the authority of the League, and, when the League has decided, regard the decision as obligatory. When a symbol is imposed on a society by recognized authority, that symbol is obligatory, though it is not indispensable or essential. To observe it is a matter of loyalty, yet the society could exist without it. To use symbol is essential to societies, but not to use any particular symbol. Particular symbols are only obligatory. [1]

A symbol, however, may become obligatory, not only by the formal decision of a society, but by mere custom. Among many peoples there is an ' unwritten law ' that a

---

[1] Perhaps two further illustrations will help to bring out clearly the important distinction between the essential and the obligatory. In every society it is obligatory that a man should have a name, but names are not essential to human nature. A nameless man would still be a man. A child is a human being before it has a name. (And if it be said that we cannot conceive of a society that did not use names, it is also true that it need not use any particular names. Cf. pp. 21 f.) The second illustration is from a story told in the *Methodist Recorder* of December 12, 1924, on the authority of Sir Henry Lunn. The story concerns the well-known Beaumont Claire, who was formerly a Roman Catholic priest. Sir Henry once asked Claire why he gave up the Roman priesthood, and this was Claire's reply : ' My old nurse came to me one day when I was in my study, and told me she had something of considerable personal interest to tell me. She said that when it was supposed that I was presented for Baptism, she had actually brought her own child. So that I, a priest, had never been baptized ! I went to Cardinal Logue and told him the story. The Cardinal said, " That is easily remedied. I will ring for some water, and then christen you, confirm you, and ordain you." " Am I to gather then," I asked, " that my Confirmation and Ordination amount to absolutely nothing ? " " Yes, indeed," said the Cardinal, " they were wholly out of order." " Then my vows are invalid," I went on. " Yes," replied the Cardinal, " entirely so." " Then I will bid you good day "—and Beaumont Claire had left the priesthood of which he had never been a " valid " member, though he had worked in it for years.' The obligatory can admit exceptions ; the essential cannot.

gentleman shall raise his hat in greeting a lady. I do not suppose that any legislature ever gravely decreed the rule, but custom makes it obligatory. Millions recognize the obligation every day. The use of another set of symbols is becoming obligatory in this way before our eyes. The coming of the motor demands it. Policeman on ' point duty ' use certain symbolic movements of the hand to direct traffic. I understand that these movements have now been imposed on the police by authority, but many an ordinary citizen, happening to stand at a cross-road, uses them to help motorists whose faces he has never seen before. Again, there has grown up a recognized set of signs by which one motorist signals to another. It has been suggested that these should be codified and imposed by law, but, apart from such formal decision, they are increasingly obligatory by custom. A difference between the two kinds of obligatory symbols emerges. The obligations imposed by the decision of recognized authority may be defined and enumerated ; those imposed by custom cannot so easily be codified. Indeed, one man's account of them would differ from another's. For instance, the symbol of the hand-shake is obligatory by custom, yet there is a considerable range of difference in men's answers to the question, ' With whom shall I use this symbol of friendliness ? ' The instance of the symbols of motoring illustrates another closely allied point. A symbol, or set of symbols, may at first be sporadic and occasional in use, confined indeed to comparatively few, who would fain be the makers of new symbolism. The society may accept their suggestions, or reject them. Or again, a symbol that has once been customary may gradually die out. At one time, for instance, to carry a sword was the mark of a gentleman. Or again, a society may use the same symbol to mean different things at different times. Erasmus tells us, in a famous passage, that he liked to come to England because there it was customary for a gentleman to greet all his lady friends with a kiss! Such was not then the custom of the Continent, and such is not the custom in England now. Again, the same symbol may mean different things in different societies. To put out the tongue is a token of impudence in England, but in some Indian sculptures a goddess is represented with her tongue hanging out in token of shame. Or again, in the famous pictures at Seringapatam, which celebrated the victory of Hyder Ali over Colonel Baillie, the captured British commander is represented as showing his mortification by sucking his thumb! It will be seen that the subject of the use of outward signs is a wide one, and has many curious corners. But we must pass to more important points. Enough has been said to show that the symbols of a living society will sometimes continue and sometimes change.

The next phenomenon to note is this—when the life of a society is healthy, the material symbol and its spiritual correlative may be so closely knit that the society's common thought and speech treat them as one. The readiest example is the use of proper names. In thought the name ' William Brown ' and a given man are treated as one, though they are not really so. It is the same with all words. If, for instance, in a home a child says to his mother, ' Father has gone out,' the mother does not stop to say to herself, ' Now that sentence is a set of sounds, and sounds are only material things, and it may be that they do not tally with those spiritual things, the thoughts in the mind of the child.' She simply assumes that the words and thoughts are so closely knit that they of course go together ; she even treats them as one. But there is a further pre-supposition—that we are speaking of a home where it is customary to tell the truth. In other words, we are speaking of a healthy society. If the people in the home were none of them truthful people, if

the child had learnt from his mother herself the habit of
lying, she might hesitate about assuming that the word
and thought were the same. And, indeed, while the
words were, ' Father has gone out,' the thought might be,
' Father is upstairs, but I want mother to think that he
has gone out.' A lie is the first of sins against symbols.
No society could exist if its members always lied to each
other. In a healthy society it is all but always a justifiable
assumption that the word and its meaning go together.
In a perfect society this would always be so. When once
a symbol has been selected, it ought to be inseparable
from its meaning, and it very often is. For instance,
among Christian people it is all but unknown that a
woman wear a plain gold ring upon the third finger of her
left hand if she is not married. Perhaps a New Testament
instance, about which there is no controversy, may be
added. Paul has this saying. ' I give you to understand
that no man speaking in the Spirit of God saith, Jesus is
anathema : and no man can say, Jesus is Lord, but in the
Holy Spirit.'[1] It is clear that Paul here does not mean
that, if a man is a true Christian, he cannot utter the
words, ' Jesus is anathema '—else every minister who has
read the verse in public worship would be a heathen !
Similarly, the Apostle does not mean that a non-Christian
cannot say the words, ' Jesus is Lord,' for multitudes of
nominal Christians have done so. In Apostolic days, to
be a Christian was so difficult that no one joined the
Christian society unless he were sincere, and Paul could
take it for granted that the man who used either phrase
meant what he said. He could assume that the symbol
and the meaning were indissolubly wedded.

In a healthy society, again, the use of a symbol may
feed or nourish the experience that it expresses.
Whenever the kiss is rightly used, it not only expresses
love but nourishes it. The same idea lies behind the

[1] I Cor. xii. 3.

saying, ' Keep your friendships in repair.' People sometimes say about a friend of long ago, ' If I were to meet
him after these twenty years, we should begin just where
we left off.' It may be doubted whether this is so. If the
two old friends met, they would probably spend a happy
hour recalling the experiences of the past, but, as soon
as they tried to face the present and its problems in the
old comradeship, each would find that the other had
changed. And if, during the twenty years, they had lived
in the same street and never ' spoken,' it is certain that
they could not begin where they left off. When fellowship is true, the use of symbols nourishes fellowship.

An obvious distinction among symbols should perhaps
be named, though it is too obvious to need prolonged
elucidation. Some symbols are signs of initiation into a
society, and therefore they normally only occur once
for any given member. Other symbols are employed in
the continuous life of the society, and may recur more or
less frequently. In the Middle Ages a man was only once
dubbed knight. To suggest the repetition of the symbol
would have been an insult. On the other hand, the use
of the hand-shake is habitual. It often follows that
there is a peculiar solemnity about the single use of a
symbol of initiation and about the rare use of a rarely
repeated symbol, which it is difficult or even impossible
to retain for the frequently repeated symbol of constant
fellowship. It would be impossible to attach to every
hand-shake the high solemnities of the dubbing of a
knight in the age of chivalry.

A curious consequence ensues. Sometimes the use of
the symbols that are meant to be repeated grows more
frequent with the deepening of fellowship and sometimes
it grows less frequent. For instance, as the friendship
between a young fellow and a girl deepens into love, their
use of the symbols of fellowship generally grows greater.
This is peculiarly true of the symbol of the kiss ! Yet,

not infrequently, when the same two people have been married forty years, they not only kiss each other less often, but the use even of words has grown less and less necessary. Each of them knows the other so intimately that often, when any subject falls under consideration, each knows what the other is thinking by the hint of a word or two, a look, or the lift of an eyebrow. Or again, if two people, knowing much of each other through the medium of writing or public repute, each come to long to meet the other, it usually happens that, when they do meet, their use of symbols of fellowship is effusive. Yet there is a famous story in the *Little Flowers of St. Francis* which tells how King Louis of France went to see Brother Giles, and how, throughout their meeting, neither saint spoke a single word. And, in answer to the expostulation of the friars when the king had gone, Giles said, ' Dear Brothers, marvel not that neither I to him nor he to me could speak a word ; sith so soon as we embraced each other, the light of heavenly wisdom revealed and showed to me his heart, and mine to him. . . . The weakness of human speech, that cannot express clearly the secret mysteries of God, would have left us all disconsolate rather than consoled ; wherefore know ye that the king departed from me with marvellous content and consolation in his soul.' [1] Yet, on first meeting, the two saints, ' kneeling down with great devotion, embraced and kissed each other, with such signs of tender love as though for long time they had been close, familiar friends,' and during the silent interview they ' continued in this embrace.' That is, there were symbols that nourished, as well as expressed, their fellowship. And, to return to the earlier example given, is it not true that the old couple, who have spent forty years together, nourish their fellowship as much or more through their spare use of symbol as a courting pair through their manifold use ?

[1] *The Little Flowers of St. Francis*, chap. xxxiv.

The rarity of the use of symbol, at least in many instances, does not make it the less effective, but the more. No doubt differences of what is called ' temperament ' play a great part here. For some people the frequent use of symbol means most, for others its rare use. In either case, however, the truth holds that, if symbol be rightly used, it feeds or nourishes the experience that it expresses.

This phenomenon perhaps reaches its culminant example in the life of societies that are both old and vigorous. If a society is healthy, one token is the value that the members set upon their membership, and this shows itself in their love for its old symbols. They know that the experience that links the society and makes it one, not only links them with its present members, but with its past members, and the repetition of the symbol that the society has used, perhaps century after century, is dear to their hearts. Because they love the society, they love its symbols. And because the spiritual experience is theirs that has been the experience of so many of their predecessors, to observe the old symbols nourishes and feeds the experience itself. Indeed, so long as the experience is there at all, the use of the symbol, especially in a gathering of the present members of the society, may rekindle the dying embers of an almost extinct enthusiasm. Logically, such a symbolic act, or series of symbolic acts, as the coronation of an English king might be carried out with an entirely new set of symbols—but life is more than logic. I have used the word ' love ' just now. Love is more than logic. Almost all the dearest symbols are old. [1] How old is the use of a ring in marriage, or the flag in battle, or the crown of kingship, or the hand-shake of friendship? The truth that in healthy societies symbols may nourish the experience

---

[1] Occasionally, however, a new symbol may become dear at a leap—as, for instance, the ' Marseillaise ' of the French Revolution, or the red shirt of the Garibaldian. In these cases the experience expressed by the symbol is peculiarly intense.

that they express, reaches its climax in the old symbols of old societies. In other words, symbols may express and mediate history.

On the other hand, in an unhealthy society the symbol may both be divorced from the mental or spiritual experience that it ought to denote, and fail to nourish the experience that it pretends to express. The first of these facts has already been illustrated to some extent. In a lie the symbol is divorced from the thought that it ought to express. When Judas kissed Jesus in the Garden of Gethsemane, his kiss was divorced from the experience of which it was once the token. There is no need to multiply instances. The truth is commonplace. Again, in an unhealthy society a symbol may not nourish the experience that it ought to express. In many a home where love is dead, the formality of the kiss has been maintained for years. If love is altogether dead, the symbol will not revive the corpse. In the Middle Ages, when the rule of the Holy Roman Emperor grew less and less real, some of the Emperors went to Italy to be crowned, while some omitted the ceremony, but no close relation can be traced between the use of the symbol and the vigour of their power. Here, too, a few illustrations suffice to suggest many more. The significant term has already been used. An ineffective symbol becomes merely formal.

It is perhaps worth while to point out that the symbolic may cease to be itself and degenerate into the formal in two distinct ways. There may be either a hypocritical or an otiose misuse of symbols. The most famous instance of the former is the Pharisaism that Jesus gibbeted. Perhaps the most signal phrase in the famous passages is, ' Who for a pretence make long prayers.' This is the deliberate misuse of symbols. But there is also another and more insidious misuse. A symbol may become merely formal by neglect as well as by deliberation

C

—that is, of course, not by the neglect of the symbol, but of the experience that it ought to express. A man may repeat the Lord's Prayer and mean nothing by it, not only if he deliberately thinks of something else while he speaks the words, but also because his mind is not on the *qui vive* while the familiar sounds escape his lips. He is almost unawares a formalist! It is probably more common for symbols to be otiose than hypocritical. In either case they have sunk into forms because the living experience that ought to correspond to them is not there.[1]

It is now possible to answer a question that naturally arises from the above discussion, What is a healthy society, and what an unhealthy one? In a healthy society there must be the two things, a common experience—or, in one word, fellowship—and a series of symbols through which the members of the society express and nourish it. Both the spiritual and the material elements are essential for health. But which of the two is the more important? Which is creative and which created? Which uses the other? For all thinkers save materialists there can only be one answer. In all true societies fellowship is primary and its symbols secondary. While, for instance, in the society called home, love always creates and uses symbols, it is independent of them all. In ancient China, we are told, there were no kisses, but surely there was love. Symbols, on the other hand, are not independent of experience. Without it they cease to be symbols and sink into forms. To employ yet another parable, no artist can do without tools, yet it is not the tools that make the artist. In the life of societies the common experience is the artist, and the symbol is the tool. The usual relation between the spiritual and the material worlds holds in the realm of

---

[1] Compare the ways in which November 5 and November 11 respectively are observed.

symbols. The spiritual is dominant and creative, the material ancillary and created. So we reach the principle that *it is spiritual experience that gives validity to symbols, and not symbols that give validity to experience.*

There may be change both in the experience of societies and in their symbols. These changes are, or ought to be, concomitant. Occasionally both experience and symbol may suffer sudden change. Or at least experience may *seem* suddenly to change, while symbol really does so, as when a heathen nation, becoming at least 'nominally' Christian, burns its idols and pulls down its temples, or in such national agonies as the French or Russian Revolution. But the normal and better way is for experience and symbol to change slowly as well as to change together. There has been gradual change in the symbolism of the Coronation of English Sovereigns through the long centuries, but it has been so gradual as hardly to be noticed. At the last two Coronations, for instance, the King's Champion, the Dymoke, has not flung his gage from his horse in Westminster Hall. Such a symbol, having become quite meaningless, quietly perishes. Meanwhile, new symbol may arise, to express something novel in the experience. For instance, in some future English Coronation, some symbolic act may be assigned to representatives of the great Dominions beyond the seas. In the story of a society that lives a long and flourishing life, both within the realm of experience and within the realm of symbol, there will be at once continuity and change. Whether the two processes are quite alike need not be further discussed. The two should accompany each other, and, to use a familiar term, should tally. Even so, however, it is the continuity in the experience that gives value to the continuity in the symbol, and it is the change in the experience that demands change in the symbol—and not vice versa.

Even though there be nothing sudden or violent in either process, it is still true that the spiritual experience is the life of the society, and the symbol its tool. Life makes symbol ; symbol at its utmost can only nourish life.

There is another side to the subject of change in symbol. Societies almost universally, or even quite universally, use symbols as *tokens of membership*. The Freemasons again furnish a ready example. Again, in many lands the members of a family express their membership by using a common surname. Or again, a man is counted an Englishman and said to belong to the English nation if he was born in England or even on a British ship. Yet the true answer to the question, ' Who belongs to this or that society ? ' is always and only, ' He who has its spirit,' or ' He who shares the common experience that is its life.' The symbol that is erected into a token, or even a test, of membership, does not make membership, but only expresses it. And, while it is easily the best device for this purpose, it notoriously fails to fulfil it perfectly. Exponents of Freemasonry tell us that its essence is brotherhood, yet they admit that there have been Freemasons who have tried to use the Order for selfish purposes. They are then false to the society, but they may still know and use the symbols of member- ship. Again, in many a society there are ' nominal ' members, as well as hypocritical ones. Nor are these the only ways in which symbols may fail to express membership. Does a daughter who marries, and thereby begins to use a new surname, cease to belong to her old family or not ? The speeches after many a wedding protest that she does not. ' Her parents,' says the giver of a toast, ' have not lost a daughter, but gained a son.' Usually all those who hold a degree at a University are counted its members, along with those who have begun the process of taking a degree—in more usual terms, the

graduates and undergraduates. But what guarantee
is there that every graduate, whose name is still on the
University list, still has the ' spirit ' of the University ?
Probably sometimes a registrar is not even sure whether
all are alive whose names appear ! In other words, the
symbol is inadequate to its task—and it would perhaps
be impossible to find an adequate one. To take an
analogous instance from Barrie's *Peter Pan* : when Peter
bids farewell to the chief of the pirates with a word about
his ' not altogether unheroic life,' the fellow cries as
he walks the plank, ' *Floreat Etona.*' I wonder what
decision the authorities of the famous school would reach
about the implied claim !

Again, it is not always true that a member of a society
has ' lost its spirit ' if he neglects the symbols of its
membership. I remember reading a story about an old
Frenchman, living in Brittany, who, when the Great
War broke out, often went to the gate of his cottage
garden and peered down the road. At length he discerned the familiar gait of a young fellow far away.
When he drew near and spoke the word ' Father,' the
old man said, ' I was expecting you.' The son had been
away in America for years, and had left the symbols of
his nationality behind. Nominally he was no Frenchman. But in August 1914 he was French. Off he set
across a ' thousand leagues of foam ' to enlist. There
were many such on both sides in the great contest.
Again, it is possible that some of the members of a society
may conscientiously object to the symbols it selects, yet
remain loyal to it. In the first centuries of our era many
a Christian, who was quite loyal to the Roman Empire,
refused to use the symbol of sacrificing to the Emperor's
statue. Here change in the symbol had failed to keep
pace with change in the society, with the dire consequence
of death. Similarly, many of the martyrs in the Marian
persecution in England died protesting their loyalty to

the queen. It is plain that in societies, and particularly in large or old societies, the common spirit may exist without the use of the symbol of membership, or the use of the symbol without the spirit. Yet the use of symbol as token of membership is not only legitimate, but useful, and perhaps even inevitable. Once more, however, the secondariness of symbol appears alongside its value. It is a tool, albeit the greatest of tools.

C. SACRAMENTAL SYMBOLS

As already stated, the preceding discussion has been conducted to prepare the way for the particular subject of the use of material media in a given society, the Church. Perhaps I may say that this has not been done in order to ' beg the question,' but merely because there are advantages in elucidating a given opinion in ' indifferent ' instances, before its controversial instance is discussed. The question now emerges, How far do the general truths about the way in which societies use the world of things, apply to the Church?

It is agreed that the Church is a society, but this, of course, does not dispose of the matter. *Genera* fall into *species*, and, not infrequently, a particular *species*, through some peculiarity, fails to display all the characteristics of the *genus*. Is there some peculiarity in the Church that invalidates or modifies the application of the principles elucidated above to this particular society? To use the terminology of logic instead of science, has the Church some *differentia* that mars the value of analogy in this instance? Though the Church may rightly be called a society, is it so different from other societies through some distinctive quality that in it the uses of the material world differ radically from those in other societies? All agree that the Church has its own *differentia*—that it is in some way unlike other societies—but there is great variety in the accounts of this *differentia*. In order to answer the above question, a writer must first give his own account of the distinctive quality of the Church. I will try to do this, again premising that my primary purpose is not to criticize or combat the accounts of others, but as clearly as may be to state my own.

There was a time when the Church might have been defined as the religious society, and this is not a bad starting-point. Yet it is manifestly insufficient for believers in immanence. To-day the belief in immanence has ceased to be merely nominal. It is taken seriously to mean that God is at work, by His Spirit, in all His universe. Christian thinkers, as well as some others, add that the Spirit of God is peculiarly and distinctively active in the world of men. Many of them go on to say that He is active in every true society—no doubt in varying ways and degrees, yet still active.[1] They do not think that the imperfections of societies altogether thwart His activity, any more than the imperfections of individual men entirely thwart His work in the individual soul. They say that the home, the nation, and the great society called mankind, that is still struggling to the birth, are all religious—or at least all may be religious, and ought to be. It is not enough, therefore, to define the Church as the religious society.

A further comparison with the work of the Holy Spirit in the individual may help. While it is the Christian doctrine that He works in the heart of every man in whom there lingers even a single holy thought or good desire, certain men are singled out as ' religious men ' because they are conscious of His work in their hearts, as others are not. Nor is this all. Not only are they conscious

---

[1] This is discussed more at large in chap. xvi. of *The Christian Experience*.

of the Holy Spirit's presence and help, they seek it and welcome it. To ' receive ' the Holy Spirit fully is the passion of their lives. It is this conscious and willing fellowship with God that marks them out as ' religious men.' A similar distinction may be made among societies. Wherever in any society there is anything good, there the Holy Spirit is at work, but often the society is not aware of this ; still less does it welcome Him ; least of all does it think of itself as existing for no other purpose than that He may perfect it, and through it mankind. In the Church there is a willing and conscious fellowship with God that makes it a ' religious society.' When at length all other societies learn that this fellowship is their life, they will blend or harmonize in a Church that is indeed universal, and indistinguishable from the Kingdom of God.

In this sense, then, the Church is a religious society. Yet this definition is inadequate, for it may be used of non-Christian religious societies. The Church is the Christian society. Its full *differentia* now appears. The Christian believes that the Spirit of God is the Spirit of Christ. He believes that the Holy Spirit was fully manifest in our Lord Jesus Christ, and that by and through Him God gives His Spirit fully to those who whole-heartedly ' ask Him.' Christian theology has rightly distinguished the Son and the Spirit, but, while it distinguishes the three Persons in the Trinity, it also declares that they are one. And at this point the unity of the Son and the Spirit is more prominent than their distinction. When Paul speaks of ' Christ in you, the hope of glory,' and of being ' led by the Spirit of God,' he refers to the same experience. Indeed, in a well-known passage he speaks in a breath of ' the Spirit of God dwelling in you,' ' Christ being in you,' and ' having the Spirit of Christ.'[1] The Church is the society that enjoys

[1] Rom. viii, 9 ff.

conscious and willing fellowship with the living Christ. Its characteristic act, therefore, is the worship of God in Christ.

There is, of course, much else to say before a complete doctrine of the Church is integrated, but this will perhaps suffice, at least at this point, and we may now pass to our particular question: How far do the principles enunciated above apply to the Church? And how far does its *differentia* invalidate them? A crucial instance at once appears. Above it was said that a society has no body, and that it can only be called a body as being organic, not as being in any literal sense material. Is this so of the Church? I think it is.

Of course, this is to take sides about the interpretation of some famous passages in Paul.[1] I do not propose to subject them to one more meticulous examination, for I have small hopes that it would be accepted. But I can indicate a general point of view. The most elaborate instance of Paul's use of this metaphor—for to me it is a metaphor—is in the Twelfth Chapter of First Corinthians. It does not seem to me possible that either here or anywhere else Paul means or says that Christians are in any material or physical sense 'members' of a 'body.' If he did mean this, then Christ must in some material or physical sense be its 'head,' and there must be some material link between Him and His followers. It will be found below that I believe that the Church uses material media, and that in a sense they may be called 'part and parcel' of the Church, but I hold that the term body, when used of the Church, is used of it in the same metaphorical way as it is used of other societies. It may be properly so used, but the meaning is not that the Church has any material counterpart, as the soul of an individual man has a material counterpart in his body. What is meant is that the Church is an organic whole—

[1] Rom. xii. 5 ; 1 Cor. xii. 20 ; Eph. i. 23, iv. 12, v. 30 ; Col. i. 24.

that its parts have a living connexion with, and relation to, each other. It is a spiritual organism. The distinctive quality of the Church, of course, here again appears, for each of its members is organically and vitally one with the Christ—and this is not so in other societies. But the sense in which the word ' body ' may be used of the Church is still the same as of other societies. An examination of the context of Paul's uses of the phrase ' the body of Christ ' seems to me to sustain this contention, and in particular an examination of the longest passage, the Twelfth Chapter of First Corinthians.[1] The Apostle is not there discussing the outward or material organization of the Church at all. He is speaking of ' spiritual gifts ' and mutual ministries. No doubt material media were used in these ministries, but it is not these that the Apostle has in view. He is explaining to the quarrelsome Corinthians that spiritually they are organically one with Christ, and therefore with each other. He is appealing to the nature of societies, and of the particular society to which they belong. The climax of his discussion is the matchless song of love. Is there anything material here? There are two other New Testament metaphors for the spiritually organic unity of the Church—a building and a vine.[2] No one suggests that these are to be taken materially or physically. It is the same with the third term, body. All three terms express the organic unity of Christians, both as individuals and as a society, with the Christ, and all have their interpretation in the deepest of all texts about the Church's unity—Christ's prayer for His people ' that they may be one, even as we are.'[3] The Father and the Son are a living unity, but they are not a material one. Like all other societies, the Church

[1] At first sight Eph. v. 28 ff. may seem an exception, but I do not think it is really so. The passage is difficult on any interpretation, but Paul cannot mean that marriage is in *every* way like the relation between Christ and the Church. They are alike on the spiritual, not the physical side. The phrase ' of His flesh and of His bones ' is, of course, not original.

[2] Eph. ii. 20 ff. ; John xv. 1 ff.   [3] John xvii. 11.

has organic unity ; like them, it uses material media ; like them, however, it has no literal ' body ' ; unlike them, its unity is consciously and adoringly with Christ.

But, while it was denied above that societies have ' bodies ' in any material sense, it was maintained that societies make a characteristic use of the material world. It provides them with the symbols that are the usual media of their fellowship. It seems to me that the Church uses the material world in this way. Yet here, too, while it is like other societies, it has its own *differentia*, its distinctive quality. Here too, again, this *differentia* springs out of the fact that the Church is the society that holds conscious and willing fellowship with the Risen Christ. He is the chief member, its ' head,' organically one with the society, ' part and parcel ' of it. Indeed, ' without Him ' it would be nothing. The Church's symbols, therefore, are symbols of an experience in which He has a share, a fellowship to which He is a party. The right term, as it seems to me, to denote this distinguishing quality in the symbols of the Church is ' Sacramental.' The Church, therefore, is the Sacramental society.

It is perhaps necessary at this point to remember that the word ' Sacramental ' has at least three meanings, which, though they are various, yet pass one into the other. It is becoming common for believers in immanence to use the term of all nature, inasmuch as all nature is, or ought to be, a medium of fellowship between God and man. For instance, God has spoken to multitudes through the beauty of the sunset. When this happens—when some are found to listen to the divine speech that is ever there—then men find, through the sunset, fellowship with God, and, as this fellowship is mediated through a material thing, the experience of such worshippers may be rightly called ' Sacramental.' This is the broadest use of the word. It is not peculiar to Christianity, for devout men of all faiths have heard God's voice in nature. The second use of the term is the one noted above. In it any material media that Christ and Christians use in fellowship, He giving and they receiving, may be called ' Sacramental.' There are illustrations in the story of Jesus' washing of the disciples' feet, and in the *sufflatio*, or ' on-breathing,' of the Twentieth Chapter of John.[1] Thirdly, the term ' Sacrament ' may, of course, be used especially of Baptism and the Lord's Supper. These two are treated separately below. Much of what is now being said applies to them, but they have also their own distinction and problems. At present the word ' Sacramental ' is being used in the second of these three senses, and under it the Church of Christ is the Sacramental society. The *differentia* of its use of symbols is that through them it enjoys conscious and willing fellowship with the living Christ.

It may conduce to clearness if I here set down as well as I can four possible opinions about the Church's use of material media. First, some might hold that the use of material media of fellowship in the Church is wholly mistaken, and that Christians should endeavour to do without them. Some mediaeval mystics seem, for instance, to have taught that the highest possible Christian state is a mystic ' vision,' in which the use of all media, even of the Eucharist[2] itself, is surpassed and needless. At the other extreme there would stand the opinion that the use of the right material *instrumentum* is the only essential. Here there is no place for the spiritual at all. It would be correct to apply the term ' magical ' or ' superstitious ' to this idea. As will appear below, it seems to me that what I call the ' Sacerdotal ' opinion has often degenerated into the ' magical,' but no Christian thinker has ever

[1] Ver. 22.

[2] I see no reason why this name for the Lord's Supper should not be used. It is only Greek for ' thanksgiving,' and who denies that in the Lord's Supper there is a ' sacrifice of praise and thanksgiving ' ? One often needs a single word to denote this Sacrament, and there does not seem to be any other so common and convenient.

advocated the latter. It is not only admitted, but asserted, by all Christian teachers, that the Church is a spiritual society, and that in it the spiritual is more important than the material. It follows, I think, that it is improper to apply the term 'magical,' as some staunch Evangelicals have done, to the Sacerdotal opinion. May I appeal to my fellow Evangelicals to cease to use so provocative a term? If we pass from these two extreme opinions, there remain two, which divide the allegiance of Christians to-day. The exponents of one of them hold that, while it is inevitable and indeed beneficial that the Church should use material symbols, no particular symbol is essential or indispensable. The exponents of the other maintain that without the use of particular material media there is no guarantee of spiritual experience in the Church. I use the name 'Sacramental' for the first of these two opinions, and the term 'Sacerdotal' for the second. I am, of course, aware that others use these terms differently, but it is convenient to have names for theories, and I hope that, having defined these terms, I may use them without offence in the sense given. I cannot honestly yield the name 'Sacramental' to the High Churchman. As I have already stated, my chief purpose is to set out the theory that I call 'Sacramental,' and not directly to controvert the theory that I call 'Sacerdotal,' but, while describing the first, I have the second also in mind. Three remarks may here be added about it. The word 'Sacerdotal,' like the word 'Sacramental,' may be used in wider and narrower ways. The definition given is one of the wider. Again, I have tried so to define the Sacerdotal opinion as to allow for the admission of some of its advocates that, through the 'uncovenanted mercies' of God, grace may be given to Christians who do not use the prescribed media, particularly if they are not to blame for their ignorance or neglect of them. In view of this admission,

I have not said that under the Sacerdotal theory the use of given media is ' essential,' but that, apart from such media, there is no *guarantee* or *certainty* of Christ's gifts of grace.

The third remark is more important. The word ' grace ' has just been used. Students of theology know that Protestant and Romanist, Evangelical and Sacerdotalist, define this word in different ways, and that the controversy about the nature of grace is intimately connected with the controversy about the Ministry and Sacraments. An attempt is being made here to discuss the latter subject separately, yet it is not possible to do so without noticing the allied controversy. For the Evangelical and Protestant, ' grace ' is a quality in God—as much so as love or holiness or omnipotence. It follows that when such a phrase is used as ' the grace of God is shed abroad in your hearts,' it is meant that God Himself is at work in ' your hearts.' In other words, while ' grace ' may be *thought of* and spoken of by itself, as we can think of such personal qualities as courage or justice alone, it cannot, and does not, *exist* alone. To exist, a quality must be the quality of some person or object. Wherever, therefore, there is grace, it is because the Holy Spirit is there. Under this meaning it is clear that there cannot be ' a higher gift than grace.' The writer of the line just quoted, however, was a Romanist. For him and other Sacerdotalists, ' grace ' is more than a quality. It is something that is itself objective, something that is ' infused ' by God into men. I do not like to say that it is semi-physical or semi-material, though it is difficult to avoid such phrases. Perhaps it is most commonly thought of as a kind of power. But the relation of the Sacramental and Sacerdotal controversy, as defined above, to the definition of grace will now be evident. When an Evangelical speaks of ' means of grace,' he intends to name the ways in which Christ holds fellowship with him.

If a Sacerdotalist uses the phrase, he intends to name the material media through which the objective thing called ' grace ' is ' infused ' by Christ into men's nature. Evangelicals claim that they use the word in Paul's way, while Sacerdotalists use it in one of Augustine's. In this Lecture the nature of grace is not under immediate discussion, but the Evangelical doctrine about it is assumed. Here grace is a quality in God ; it is His love as it shows itself confronting sin ; it is His love as seen in Christ. Such a phrase as ' By *grace* are ye saved ' is parallel to Paul's other phrase, ' The *peace* of God . . . shall guard your hearts,' or Ignatius' saying, ' The *love* of the brethren . . . greets you.'[1] All such phrases use the names of qualities for the persons who exercise the qualities. Where there is grace, God Himself is present, for a person's quality cannot be where He is not.[2]

We may now ask how far the phenomena of symbols, as they occur in other societies, occur also in the Church. These phenomena have been described in the previous section of the chapter. It is necessary to select some of the many symbols that have been used in the Church as examples. Those named in the New Testament will best serve the purpose. In addition to the two Sacraments of Baptism and the Lord's Supper, the following symbols are found—the ' laying on of hands,' later called, in one of its instances, Ordination ; the ' breathing ' of the Risen Christ upon the Apostles, technically called the *sufflatio*[3] ; the washing of feet[4] ; the ' right hand of fellowship '[5] ; the ' holy kiss '[6] ; the ' lifting up of hands.'[7] Some would add ' unction ' or

---

[1] *Philad.* xi. 2.

[2] The term ' gift ' (of grace) ($\chi \acute{a} \rho \iota \sigma \mu a$) approximates rather more closely to what a Sacerdotalist means by ' grace ' ($\chi \acute{a} \rho \iota s$), yet even it is not anything external to a Christian's personality, but the result of the influence or operation of the grace of the Indwelling Christ upon the particular personality of a particular Christian.

[3] John xx. 22.   [4] John xiii. 1 ff.   [5] Gal. ii. 9.
[6] Rom. xvi. 16 f   [7] Luke xxiv. 50 ; 1 Tim. ii. 8.

'anointing with oil,' but it may be that, where there is reference to a literal anointing, a medical remedy is meant, and not a symbolic act.[1] It will be remembered that the 'laying on of hands' has several different uses—Jesus 'laid His hands' on children in blessing[2]; He 'laid hands on' sick folk in miracles of healing[3]; on two occasions we are told that, after Baptism, Apostles 'laid their hands' on converts and 'they received the Holy Ghost'[4]; a passage in the Epistle to the Hebrews probably refers to this use, and, if so, it implies that this was not exceptional, but customary, in the Church'[5]; the 'laying on of hands' was also used sometimes in Apostolic times when particular disciples were set apart for some particular work—the Apostles 'laid their hands' on the Seven, usually called 'deacons'[6]; the 'prophets and teachers' at Antioch 'laid their hands' on Barnabas and Saul when they 'sent them' on their First Missionary Journey[7]; finally there are the three famous references in the Pastoral Epistles,[8] of which more is said below. Prayer is the usual accompaniment of the 'laying on of hands.' The 'lifting up of hands' is symbolic of supplication in one passage,[9] and of benediction in another.[10]

In discussing these symbols, it will perhaps be best to begin by exhibiting the points of agreement between the Sacramental and Sacerdotalist opinions, as above defined, and then to state what I take to be the Sacramental position about points of difference. In pursuing this line of thought, one or two general remarks will first be made. Then there follows an application of the principles enunciated in the last section in various New Testament instances. The Sacraments of Baptism and the Lord's Supper and the symbol of the Laying On of Hands, however, are reserved for separate treatment.

---

[1] Mark vi. 13 ; Jas. v. 14 f. ; cf. Luke x. 34.   [2] Mark x. 16.
[3] Mark v. 23.   [4] Acts viii. 17, xix. 6.   [5] Heb. vi. 2.
[6] Acts vi. 6.   [7] Acts xiii. 3.   [8] 1 Tim. iv. 14, v. 22 ; 2 Tim. i. 6.
[9] 1 Tim. ii. 8.   [10] Luke xxiv. 50.

About the other symbols there seems to me to be a large degree of agreement ; about these three there is, of course, difference. Only one of them is discussed in this chapter. At the end of this section I take the Laying On of Hands as an example of the difference between the Sacramentalist and Sacerdotalist.

We begin, then, with two general remarks. First, it is noteworthy that many of the New Testament symbols were borrowed from the Jews. It is not possible to quote exact Old Testament parallels to the use of feet-washing as a symbol of humility, but, in societies where the cleansing of sandalled feet fell universally to the lower kind of bondman, it was almost inevitable that this symbol should be used by conquerors and despots.[1] Again, there is perhaps no exact Old Testament parallel for the symbolic ' breathing ' of the Twentieth Chapter of John, but the breath is an almost universal symbol for ' spirit,' or, rather, among many peoples the breath was at first identified with the spirit, and it was only at a later stage that the first became a mere metaphor for the second. Both stages of early thinking are traceable in the Old Testament. The New Testament all but says outright that the custom of baptism was accepted by our Lord from John. In the Sacrament of the Lord's Supper many find a reference to the ritual of the Passover, though they add that the distinction is more important than the likeness. Below, the ritual of the Lord's Supper is referred to a much commoner symbol. All other symbols named—the ' laying on of hands,' the ' lifting up of hands,' the ' holy kiss,' the ' right hand of fellowship '— have anticipations in the Old Testament, and were clearly borrowed from the environment of the early Church, though, of course, they were all given a distinctively Christian meaning.

Second, it is clear that the Church, like other societies,

[1] Cf. Ps. lx. 8.

D

was obliged to use symbols. As already seen, at the least it could not do without the symbols of speech. But the Church not only used the symbols that it could not avoid ; it did not hesitate to use symbols whenever they served its turn. There is no hint of objection to their use at all, but just the same simple acceptance of these media of fellowship as occurs elsewhere. When, for instance, our Lord wished to preach a sermon by action, He ' began to wash the disciples' feet ' ; or again, when ' James and Cephas and John ' wished to express their recognition of the apostolate of Paul and Barnabas, they gave them the ' right hand of fellowship ' as naturally as other men would use the same symbol to express other kinds of fellowship. There is no need to labour this point. The Church used symbols just as inevitably and willingly as other societies have always done.

To pass to the five symbols about whose use and value there is general agreement—the *sufflatio*, the feet-washing, the ' right hand of fellowship,' the ' holy kiss,' and the ' lifting up of hands '—it is not difficult to show that the phenomena of symbols named in the last section obtain of them, and that, in addition, they have the Christian *differentia*, and were, in the sense named, Sacramental.

It will be agreed, first, that none of these is essential to the Christian society. There is none of them that has not been used in some subsequent era of the Church, but there is no claim that they have been universal or ought to have been—in other words, there is no claim that they are essential. The *sufflatio*, for instance, is still used in the Ordination of a bishop in the Coptic Church. Or again, year by year the Pope washes the feet of twelve poor men on Maundy Thursday ; some monarchs, as the Austrian Emperors, have also followed this use. Yet no one would say that these symbols are essential to the Church. Tolstoy tells us, in his *Resurrection*, that

the custom of the 'holy kiss' on Easter Day survives in the Russian Church, but no one pretends
that the churches of other lands had no right to
discontinue it. The use of the symbol of the 'right
hand of fellowship' has often obtained in the Church ; it
is used, for instance, in the Wesleyan Service for the
Recognition of Members ; but there is no claim that it is
the necessary guarantee of the validity of any ritual. The
Church has passed from the 'lifting up of hands,' as the
usual sign of supplication, to kneeling before God, without
any serious protest.

Again, an examination of these symbols illustrates the
distinction between the terms 'essential' and 'obligatory.' Though none of them is essential in the Church,
yet the 'holy kiss' would beo bligatory in the churches
to whom Paul wrote, 'Salute one another with an holy
kiss,' for these churches were those at Rome, Corinth, and
Thessalonica, and they all admitted the authority of the
great Gentile Apostle. Again, in the Apostolic Church
the use of the 'lifting up of hands' and the 'right hand of
fellowship' would be obligatory in the second sense of the
term distinguished above—they would be obligatory, so
far as we can judge, not by the direct command of any
recognized authority, but by the authority of custom,
like the symbol of kneeling in prayer to-day. Yet it is
to be noted that, though there is direct and repeated
Apostolic command for the use of the 'holy kiss,' the
Church of later days has thought itself at liberty to
abandon the symbol—of course, because it is used in
modern societies as symbol of other things than Christian
fellowship. It follows that, at least in some instances,
an Apostolic injunction is not held to be perpetually
obligatory. In a not dissimilar way, the Church has taken
upon itself to decide that when our Lord Himself said,
after washing the disciples' feet, 'I have given you an
example, that ye should do as I have done to you,' He

meant that His followers should imitate His humility, without repeating the symbol of it. It is agreed by Christians, with practical unanimity, that the Church rightly makes this distinction. It follows that the Church is like other societies, both in declaring some things that are not essential to be none the less obligatory, and in varying these from time to time.[1]

Further, these symbols illustrate the truth that in a healthy society a symbol and the experience that it symbolizes may be so wedded in thought and use that the one implies the other. For instance, it is obvious that when the older Apostles gave Paul and Barnabas the ' right hand of fellowship ' the experience of fellowship and its symbol were so well knit that they could be spoken of as a single thing. Or again, the ' holy kiss ' of the first Christians would not be only formal, still less treacherous, like the kiss of Judas. Holy love and its symbol would go as naturally together as a word and its meaning. The Church had this mark of a vigorous and living society. The supreme instances, of course, are in the story of our Lord Himself. When He washed His disciples' feet, who could sever the symbol from its meaning? Surely the two were blent, again, when He laid hands on the children or the sick. It is not so obvious, however, that, when He used these symbols of fellowship, the suitable experience was always present in those for whom He used them. The clearest instance is in the story of the feet-washing. Just as Jesus finished the hallowed task, He said, ' Ye are clean, but not all.' And presently Judas, ' having received the sop, went

---

[1] Some other variations from biblical precedent may be named—the Fasting Eucharist, the Mixed Chalice, the separation of Baptism and Confirmation, the disuse of immersion in Baptism, and so on. Other symbols have, of course, been added. A Methodist lady, visiting York, wrote as follows to a friend: ' One afternoon I was sitting alone in the minster, lost in amazement at the beauty of the " Five Sisters " window, when very gently the Lord drew near, stood by me, and for a few moments we communed together as a man with his friend.'

out straightway.'[1] Clearly Jesus had washed Judas'
feet, among the rest, but for him the symbol meant
nothing, or worse. The symbol and the experience it
was meant to recall and feed were divorced. The seen
and the unseen fell asunder ; their proper unity was
lost. A different kind of example emerges when we
read that Jesus, after His Resurrection, ' breathed on '
the disciples, and said, ' Receive ye the Holy Spirit.'
To us the symbol and the experience may here be one in
thought, for we may hold that the experience began at
the moment when the symbol was used. But, at the
least, it was not complete till a later date, when ' the
Day of Pentecost was now come.' This instance illustrates the ease with which a symbol and its corresponding
experience may blend in thought, yet be separate in fact.

It is plain, again, that these symbols, when rightly
used, not only expressed the experience that they represented, but nourished or fed it. The instances of the
sufflatio and the feet-washing only need again to be
named. All the disciples, except Judas, rose from the
table in the Upper Room, not only with cleansed feet,
but with humbler hearts. All the disciples left the
Upper Room of the Resurrection days readier for the
Holy Spirit. So, too, the giving of the ' right hand of
fellowship ' warmed the hearts of the Jewish and Gentile
Apostles to one another ; the ' holy kiss ' nourished the
fellowship of the first Christians, as well as expressed it.
Again, the later history of these symbols illustrates the
value in long-lived societies of using historic symbols.
It is not likely that, if a new symbol of humility were
sought to-day by the Pope, he would select feet-washing,
but to use it links him with the long line of earlier Popes,
and illustrates for many a devout Roman Christian the
unity of the present with the lengthening past. It may
be that if the Russian Church were seeking a new emblem

[1] John xiii. 10, 30.

of fellowship for Easter Day, it would not select the ' holy kiss,' but the historic symbol links every new Easter with the multitude gone. Such symbols are not essential to the continuity of the life of the Church, but admirably express it, and, in expressing, strengthen it. Once more, it is clear that if any of these emblems became what is clumsily called a ' mere symbol '—that is, if it ceased to be a real symbol and became a form—its efficacy would lapse. And this would be so, whether, as in the instance of Judas' kiss, it were used with deliberate deceit, or whether, as probably began to happen with the ' holy kiss ' in the quarrelsome Corinthian Church, it gradually and without premeditation began to be less and less really symbolic and more and more nearly formal.

To sum up, it appears to be clear that in these instances the usual phenomena that attend the use of material media in societies occur, and that the general principle is true of them—it is the experience symbolized that validates the symbol, and not the symbol that ensures the experience. Again, it seems clear that the symbol is not needed even to guarantee the experience. No one suggests that those who do not use these symbols are abandoned to ' uncovenanted mercies.' So much seems to be agreed.

But another question now arises : Can these symbols rightly be called Sacramental? Or, to put the same question in another way : Had the grace of our Lord Jesus Christ any place in them? Under the definitions of ' Sacramental ' and ' grace ' submitted above, it seems that the answer is ' Yes.' For a symbol was said to be Sacramental when it denoted an experience in which the living Christ had a part, or, more exactly, an experience in which the Church, or some of its members, consciously and willingly shared with Him. Under this definition, all the symbols named are Sacramental. There is no need to illustrate this for the feet-washing and the *sufflatio*, or for Christ's ' lifting up of hands ' in blessing, in their first instances, for He Himself did these things. When they are repeated by Christians in later times, it is still true, though not so obvious, that our Lord plays a part. If a Pope were to wash the feet of twelve poor men, without any thought of Christ, his act would not be Sacramental. But when he washes their feet, it is surely with the prayer, ' O Christ, teach me in this act to remember and practise humility.' Christ answers sincere prayers for spiritual gifts, and in and through the symbol He teaches and helps the Pope. He Himself is present in the service of the feet-washing, and, being present, shows His love to this one of His servants— or, to use the commoner word, His fellowship shows itself in grace. ' Grace ' is the name for Christ's activity, not for a something separate from His personality that He bestows as men bestow food or clothing or other things. Similarly, whenever the ' holy kiss ' was rightly used, it denoted a fellowship of Christian with Christian on the very ground that each had fellowship with the living Christ, and their fellowship with each other was nourished by their common fellowship with Him. [1] This too, there-fore, was a Sacramental symbol ; in it, too, a present Christ gave grace to His disciples. It would be easy to show that He had a share in a similar way when the ' right hand of fellowship ' or the ' lifting up of hands ' was, or is, rightly used. These New Testament symbols were Sacramental and true ' means of grace ' because they were practised in a society that exhibited, not only the characteristics of all societies, but also its own distinctive quality, its *differentia*, conscious and willing fellowship with the living Christ.

To turn now to the symbol of the Laying On of Hands, there are some points on which there is a great degree of agreement. When our Lord ' laid His hands ' upon the

[1] Cf. 1 John i. 3.

children, He used a symbol that answers to the account given above. When, in later days, aged Christians have used the same symbol in their intercourse with little children, few will deny that, according to their smaller measure, they have used it aright and effectively. Again, the Laying On of Hands was used by our Lord in healing the sick,[1] and also by the Apostles.[2] Not a few Christians to-day claim that the Church has a ministry of healing, which it has too long largely neglected. It is noticeable that some of those who are reverently seeking again to practise this ministry use the New Testament symbol. This is right and wise, for the ancient symbol recalls the ancient ministry. It would not be difficult here, too, to apply much of what was said above about the general use of symbols in societies, and the specific use of Sacramental symbols in the Church. Probably no one would claim more for this particular instance of the Laying On of Hands. It is not suggested, for instance, that, if this symbol had been practised generation by generation, a particular 'grace' would thereby have been handed on to certain Christians, and that this grace was lost because the symbol was not so used. In other words, it is not suggested that the symbol is essential to the ministry of healing, nor that without it there is no guarantee of the efficacy of this kind of ministry. The same is true of a third New Testament use of this symbol—its use when some particular Christians were selected for a particular piece of work. The classic instance of this tells that the 'prophets and teachers' at Antioch 'laid their hands' on Paul and Barnabas when they were 'sent' on their First Missionary Journey. Some scholars—as, for instance, Dr. Hort—think that the references to the laying of hands on Timothy belong here,[3] but I prefer to yield as much as possible to my opponents, and to take them as referring to his Ordination, in the later sense of that word.

[1] Mark v. 23, &c.   [2] Acts xxviii. 8.   [3] 1 Tim. iv. 14 ; 2 Tim. i. 6.

They are, therefore, considered below. The same course is taken with the story of the Seven ' Deacons.' [1] As for the story of the sending of Paul and Barnabas, most students will agree that it illustrates the account of Sacramental symbols given above. The Church has not felt bound to follow the Apostolic precedent in this instance, and to dispatch missionaries, and others to whom special work is committed, with an imposition of hands. It is of interest to Methodists that Wesley seems to have had this story in mind when he, with other presbyters, commissioned Dr. Coke for his great work in America by this symbol, for of course Coke was already himself an ordained presbyter of the Church of England. There may, however, be some Sacerdotalists who would say that, while the laying of hands on Paul and Barnabas illustrates all the phenomena of Sacramental symbols named above, it also illustrates another—the transmission of ' grace,' under their definition of the last term. This, however, is best discussed in its better-known instances.

There remain two other New Testament uses of the Laying On of Hands, later known technically as Confirmation and Ordination. Each of them claims to find precedent in the New Testament—Confirmation in Acts viii. 17, xix. 6 ; Heb. vi. 2 ; and perhaps i Tim. v. 22 ; Ordination in i Tim. iv. 14 ; 2 Tim. i. 6 ; and (according, at least, to many authorities) in Acts vi. 6 and i Tim. v. 22. They may be considered separately.

Of the four possible references to Confirmation, two do no more than tell us that the Laying On of Hands was practised. The other two are those in the Acts of the Apostles, and run as follows : ' Now when the Apostles which were at Jerusalem heard that Samaria had received the word of God, they sent unto them Peter and John : who, when they were come down, prayed for them, that they might receive the Holy Ghost : for as yet He was

[1] Acts vi. 6.

fallen upon none of them : only they had been baptized into the name of the Lord Jesus. Then laid they their hands on them, and they received the Holy Ghost. Now when Simon saw that through the laying on of the Apostles' hands the Holy Ghost was given, he offered them money . . . '[1]; ' And Paul said [unto certain disciples at Ephesus, who had only been baptized into John's baptism], John baptized with the baptism of repentance, saying unto the people, that they should believe on Him which should come after him, that is, on Jesus. And when they heard this, they were baptized into the name of the Lord Jesus. And when Paul had laid his hands upon them, the Holy Ghost came on them ; and they spake with tongues, and prophesied.'[2]

Here there are three things pertinent to the present inquiry—Baptism, Confirmation, and the receiving of the Holy Spirit. It may be added that the term ' grace ' does not occur. The relation of the passages to Baptism will be discussed later. In regard to what has long been called Confirmation, I should myself claim that the passages illustrate and conform to the phenomena of the use of symbols by societies in general, and the use of Sacramental symbols by the Church in particular, set out above. The Apostles used an old and suitable symbol, giving it a Christian meaning. It symbolized a certain experience, and, in expressing, nourished it. It seems to me, too, that the symbol is one that might well be used in later days by the Church, and I have no doubt that, in multitudes of instances, it has in later times, not only symbolized a given experience, but been its very vehicle. Indeed, I have no doubt that, alike in the Apostolic instances and in many later ones, the experience and its symbol have been so closely knit as to be indissoluble—as indissoluble as a word and its meaning. The very phraseology of the passages shows this. For the writer

[1] Acts viii. 14–18.   [2] Acts xix. 4–6.

the two things were as inevitably one as the giving of the ' right hand of fellowship ' was one with the experience of fellowship itself, or the ' holy kiss ' one with Christian love. But, while the Laying On of Hands was the concomitant of the receiving of the Spirit, it was not its cause. Nor, again, was the symbol needed as the guarantee of the experience. For there are other instances of the receiving of the Holy Spirit where this symbol is not found.[1] It seems to me that if Luke thought of the Laying On of Hands as essential to the experience, or even as an authoritative guarantee of it, he would certainly have named it in such instances. Again, the experience itself is defined as ' receiving the Holy Spirit,' and not as the receiving of ' grace.' As already stated, to ' receive the Holy Spirit ' is to receive the Risen Christ. The Acts prefers the former phrase. Under either phrase however, God Himself entered the heart of the believer. On so entering, He would indeed give of His grace—but of His grace in the sense of the word preferred above. There is no hint that some entity, which can be considered as separable from the presence of God, was given to the believer. Grace, on the contrary, is a quality in God. As present in the heart, His personality influenced the personality of the disciple. This is His way of giving grace. There is no suggestion in the passages of the later Augustinian notion of *gratia*. It follows, of course, that neither is there anything of the notion that there was to be some such thing transmitted from the Apostles to other men, later called bishops, and that the Confirmation of such bishops was for ever to be needed as a guarantee of the ' receiving of the Holy Spirit.' Such an idea seems to me to be not only absent from the New Testament, but alien to its whole spirit. More will be said about this in a later chapter. Meanwhile, I can only say that the whole evidence for the Sacerdotal doctrine of Confirmation

[1] e.g. Acts ii. 4, x. 44.

in the New Testament is two phrases in the Book of the Acts, which admit of another and better explanation. What biblical reason is there for distinguishing this symbol from the others discussed above? I may be asked whether, if I admit that often the symbol has been of beneficial use, I should object to its being used in my own church to-day, or in a reunited Church to-morrow. The answer is that I should not object to the use of the symbol if it were once rid of the Sacerdotal notion that some find to be its deepest meaning. If this notion were abandoned, I think that the use of so historic a symbol would not only be tolerable, but desirable. Meanwhile, it seems to me that my own church is well within its rights in preferring the 'giving of the right hand of fellowship' in its Service for the Recognition of New Members, which in some ways corresponds to Confirmation, to the Laying On of Hands.

To pass to the four passages quoted under Ordination, the only noteworthy point about the earliest [1] is that men were chosen for Ordination who were already 'full of the Spirit.' [2] The other three passages are: 'Neglect not the gift that is in thee, which was given thee by prophecy, with the laying on of the hands of the presbytery' [3]; 'Lay hands hastily on no man' [4]; 'For the which cause I put thee in remembrance that thou stir up the gift of God, which is in thee through the laying on of my hands.' [5] As already stated, I waive the question whether there is here a reference to Ordination, in our sense of the word, or not. I waive also the question whether Paul wrote the Pastoral Epistles or not. Perhaps, too, there is no need to linger further over the term 'gift,' or 'gift of grace,' which occurs in two of the passages. [6] The principal question is whether these brief references can bear the weight of the theory that is built upon them. The only

---

[1] Acts vi. 6.   [2] Acts vi. 3.   [3] 1 Tim. iv. 14.   [4] 1 Tim. v. 22.
[5] 2 Tim. i. 6.   [6] See footnote on p. 47.

direct biblical evidence for the *perpetual* transmission of grace—for the idea that the Apostles transmitted to bishops a certain *gratia*, which was in turn to be transmitted to others, and that this transmission was to be integral to the Christian Church until ' the end of the days ' —is these words : ' Lay hands hastily on no man ' ! It is claimed that this shows that what Paul ' transmitted ' to Timothy, Timothy ' transmitted ' to others. It is surely remarkable that in all the literature of the New Testament there is no other or clearer reference to this cardinal point. [1] Again, of the other two texts, one definitely refers to the Laying On of Hands as the accompaniment of the ' gift,' and not as its cause, or even as its vehicle. Ought not those who lay so much stress on these texts to stress equally the fact that they state that the ' gift ' came ' by prophecy ' ? The text most commonly quoted by Sacerdotalists, however, is the passage in the Second Epistle to Timothy—' The gift of God, which is in thee through the laying on of my hands.' The reader will be prepared for the suggestion that here, too, we have only one more instance of that marriage between symbol and experience which is ideal and which obtains in healthy societies. In the Wesleyan Methodist Church, Ordination by the Imposition of Hands has been the rule since 1836—that is, it has been obligatory, though not essential. If it were now regarded as essential, we should need to repudiate the ministry of all those many Methodist ministers before that date who were not ordained in this way. The Sacerdotalist, however, is of course bound to

[1] Of course other questions arise too, as has often been urged. For instance, as neither the original Twelve nor Matthias seem to have been ordained, is there any proof that every other minister of Christ named in the New Testament (e.g. Apollos—Acts xviii. 24 ff.) was set apart by Ordination ? Or, where is the evidence that transmission was to be through *bishops* ? Or, inasmuch as the Anglican Church permits laymen to share in every duty of the Ministry except the administration of the Sacraments, where is the biblical evidence that the transmitted *gratia* related to these ? The fact is that the theory of Apostolical Succession derives its strength by its appeal, not to the Bible, but to later Church History.

deny the validity of the ' orders ' of all Methodist ministers alike—except a very few at the first, who were Anglican clergymen—because they have none of them been ordained by bishops. Yet many and many a Methodist minister could use Paul's very words about his Ordination. In ' that high hour ' a ' gift of grace ' came upon him ' through the laying on of hands.' In a healthy society that is sure to be so. The symbol is the vehicle or means of the ' gift.' Yet it is not its ground or cause or guarantee. As soon as such terms are used about symbols, it seems to the Evangelical that the symbolic begins to usurp the primacy of the spiritual, and, in usurping, to have lost its own value. There is no need to show how all the uses of symbols, as traced above, occur in the instance of Ordination. To call it a ' mere symbol ' is only to confuse the issue. There is no such thing as ' mere symbol.' If I am asked whether, as belonging to a Church that already uses Ordination, and as recognizing, besides, the value of historic symbols, I should demur to the use of Episcopal Ordination in a reunited Church, I can only say that it seems to me that the distinction between the Sacramental and Sacerdotal opinions is so important that it is not possible to allow ambiguity about the meaning of Ordination. If, therefore, the historic use of Episcopal Ordination is to obtain in a reunited Church, there should be some clear token that the Sacerdotal opinion is repudiated. To admit the present ministers of the Free Churches into the united Church as its Ministers, without Re-ordination, would be such a token.

D. The Place of Symbols in History

In the earlier part of this chapter some references were made to the importance of historic symbols. When the symbols of the Church are considered, the subject is

so important as to demand separate treatment. The
exponents of Sacerdotalism, with others, use such phrases
as 'the historic episcopate,' and 'the Apostolical succession,' and 'the principle of continuity,' and all of these
imply an appeal to the verdict of history. They claim
that the symbols used by Anglicans have been used by
the Church for many ages. They claim also that through
the same ages their theory has been held by the Church.
They add that mere historical continuity is at least one
of the tests of truth. They appeal also to the rightful
authority of the age-long Church to decide doctrine.
Some of them seem almost to postulate the infallibility
of the Church. No doubt there are differences among
them on such points, but they all agree in appealing to
history. They say that, compared with the 'Catholic
Church,' the Nonconformist 'sects' are but of yesterday.
'Schism' and error are for them inseparable, because
'schism' is a breach with history. For their own Church
they claim unbroken historic continuity with our Lord
Himself.

It does not belong to the present subject to discuss all
the manifold questions here raised. It is plain that they
cover a much wider area than the examination of the place
of symbols in the Church, yet that the problem of symbols
is involved. Even within the narrower range of this
problem the history of symbols is here omitted. Yet it
is necessary to say something about the general question
of the place of symbols in history, and to define one's
attitude to the historic claim. I may mention two reasons
for this need. First, I am among those to whom the appeal
of the historic is very strong. For instance, I can never
stand in an old church but its spell falls upon me. Then,
the appeal to history is a reasonable one. I do not
believe in the infallibility of the Church at any period.
I do not think that there is anything infallible but God.
He has been pleased to set us, for our discipline, to live in

a world where ' probability,' in Butler's famous phrase, is ' the very guide of life.' But I admit that there is great weight in the argument that it is very improbable that the Christian Church should make a mistake and continue in it for a thousand years. I believe, however, that, broadly speaking, this is just what has happened with the question at issue—that, apart from the protest of individuals and minorities, the Church went astray and became corrupt because it misunderstood and misused its symbols. Yet, at the same time, I believe that there is continuity in the history of the Church. Indeed, I believe that, if historical continuity with the historic Jesus were ever lost, there could not be a Church at all. I believe that both the ' living Christ ' and the ' Jesus of History ' are necessary to the Church in all its epochs. Or rather, I believe that these two are one. In other words, the Church is a society that has had a continuous life for nineteen centuries, and it will have a similarly continuous life until the Kingdom of God comes. To discuss all that is here involved, as I have already said, is beyond the scope of this Lecture. But the question emerges : What account does an Evangelical Christian, who holds such opinions, give of the place of symbols and Sacraments in the history of the Church ?

It will again be easiest to make my answer clear if I take first an example from outside the realm of the immediate controversy. The Church of Christ is an historic society. Are there any other historic societies whose history may be used by way of analogy ? It will perhaps serve best not to examine many, but to select one. The most famous society, after the Church, is the nation. Each of the great nations has lived for centuries. They too can claim historic continuity. They too can claim that convictions attained in their lengthened past are not likely to be mistaken. What is the place of symbols in the history of nations ?

This question needs to be approached by way of another : What is it that gives continuity to the life of a nation ? And this runs easily into the difficult question : What is a nation ? To this several answers have been given. The readiest—and to the ' man in the street ' the obvious—answer to-day is, ' A nation is a society of people who share in a common government.' With this answer it is sometimes possible to point to a definite historical event as the birthday of a nation. The United States could point to the day of the signing of the Declaration of Independence, Switzerland to the day when the famous Oath of the Rütli was taken. Yet some historians would claim, and with good grounds, that there is a sense in which there was an American nation before the Declaration was signed and a Swiss nation before the Oath was taken. And for other nations, such as the English, there is no such historical birthday at all. Further, there have been nations that were not under a single government. For instance, there was an Italian nation for more than a thousand years, even though Italy was divided into a number of different political units. A second answer makes the possession of a given country the mark of a nation. This serves well in many instances, but it fails with others—as, for instance, with the Jew or the Goth. Again, some would point to the use of a common speech as distinguishing a nation, but this would mean that the Province of Montreal is not part of the British Empire or even of Canada, and that the Swiss, with their four languages, are not a nation at all. Under a fourth suggestion, common blood or race is made the definition of a nation, but many of the great nations—as the Roman and the English—were originally of mixed descent, and there is no community of blood in such a nation as the United States. Again, in very early times a nation was one if its people worshipped the same god, but, as monolatry passed into monotheism, this kind of unity

E

failed to distinguish nations, and no one would apply this account to them to-day.

We are driven back, therefore, upon another account. It will have been noticed that all the links of nationhood so far named belong to the realm of the external. They all fall under the head of ' material things.' There are historians who claim that, while some or all of these are convenient historical marks of national unity, yet none of them, nor even all of them taken together, rightly defines a nation. They claim that essentially national unity is a psychological thing, that it belongs to the world of the unseen and spiritual, not the world of the outward and material. Here, of course, there is an instance of the unsolved mystery named at the beginning of the book. No one has yet been able to define exactly the spiritual entity that makes a nation, still less to explain the relation of this entity to a nation's land and speech and so on. None the less it seems to me that a nation, like other societies, is a society because its members share a 'common spirit,' and that the historic continuity of nations depends upon the continuity of this ' common spirit ' from generation to generation.

Another question properly follows : ' But we have no experience of such a " spiritual entity " apart from some material manifestation of it ; indeed, we cannot have such an experience ; with such a psychological phenom-enon there always goes, and there must always go, some-thing outward, something that manifests itself in the material world ; indeed, it is this latter that is usually called " historical " ; what then is the outward or material counterpart of this spiritual entity ? ' The answer that seems to me the true one is: ' A given kind of behaviour.' Here, again, definition is difficult, and so far it has proved beyond the powers of historians. I use the word ' behaviour ' for lack of a better. Yet there is a certain kind of behaviour that is characteristic of the English

nation, for instance, which can be seen both in the
' corporate ' acts of the nation and in the manifold
individual acts of its several members. In other words,
character, in nations as in individuals, has two sides,
inward and outward, spiritual and material, and these two
go together. Where the first is, there also is the second.
There is such a thing as a continuity of the English nation
—a continuity that is primarily to be defined as continuity
of spiritual experience—and this inevitably shows itself
in continuity of English behaviour. Neither of these
two can be accurately defined, yet they go to the ' root
of the matter.' Also, they are not really two, but one.
To use an old metaphor, they are like the concave and
convex of a curve.

We can now return to the accounts of the nature and
continuity of nations that have been commoner—to such
things as a common government, a common speech, a
common blood, a common land. These material things are
useful as means to express and nourish the fundamental
common experience. This is obviously true of all but a
common blood, and, when men speak of this, they do not
refer merely to physical blood, but to all that comes
to men by heredity—for many things do come by
heredity, however men of science may dispute about the
way in which this happens. When the phrase is so interpreted, it falls into line with the other three. It is clear
that here we are again upon an example of a truth already
elucidated. None of these material things is essential
to a nation's life ; none of them rightly defines it ; yet
all may express and nourish it. One instance must
suffice. At first sight, it may seem that a common land
can do none of these things. But then we listen to Hardy
singing, ' England, my England ! ' Or we remember
Stevenson's story of the way in which men of the Black
Watch, returning to Scotland after many years' service
abroad, fell on their faces and kissed the soil. The

relation between outward and inward holds still when applied to the subject of historical continuity.

Yet none of the four outward things so far named is usually called symbolic, though all of them have often been used in a symbolic way. When something is needed to serve for a nation the purposes that ritual serves for the Church, recourse is had to other things. There is a ritual of nations. Among its commonest symbols are the singing of national anthems, the use of national flags, and the repetition of national ceremonies, such as the coronation of kings. The Englishman treats these things in two ways—he depreciates them in speech, yet loves them in his heart. It is his heart that is right. The use, for instance, of a national flag does not make men English, but the habit both expresses and nourishes the common experience that is ' England.' Otherwise a poet could not have stirred so many hearts by writing, however mistakenly, of

> The flag that's braved a thousand years
> The battle and the breeze.

It is always an error to underrate the symbolic, though it is a greater to misunderstand it.

Another remark is germane to the subject of the historical continuity of the Church. If any one wished to illustrate the continuity of the English nation through many generations, to what would he turn? Probably to the list of English kings. This is the readiest token of the continuity of the nation. Yet it is not the only token. Another way would be to take the inquirer to see an old English cathedral, another to point to the unbroken retinue of English literature, another to exhibit a series of English coins, and so on. All of these are convenient tokens of the historical continuity of a certain thing that can only be called ' the English experience.' All are useful, but none is indispensable. Otherwise, to take only the line of kings, the English nation would have lapsed in the days of Oliver Cromwell, and the French nation have perished at the Revolution. In the history of nations everything outward or material or physical is secondary and ancillary. Something spiritual is primary. Granted this, the importance of the outward is great indeed. I have drawn this out in the instance of the nation, but it seems to me true, *mutatis mutandis*, of all true societies. It seems to me to be true of the Church. Here, however, the phrase *mutatis mutandis* has a special significance. There are important differences between a nation and the Church. It does not seem to me, however, that these differences destroy the analogy between the two in relation to symbols. It is necessary to show what I mean a little more fully.

First, the historic continuity of the Church depends upon the continuity of the Christian experience of fellowship with the living Christ. There is a normative account of this in the New Testament,[1] and one of the wonders of history is the way in which generation by generation the Christian experience there described is repeated. There has been no breach in this continuity since the Day of Pentecost. Also, it seems to me that no Christian has ever reached this experience alone. It has always been mediated to him in some way by the Church—if it be only that the Church has kept the New Testament for him through so many centuries, or that the Church taught his mother to teach him to pray. Continuity, in the Church as in other societies, is continuity of experience.

Yet, here too, the demand for some outward expression of this experience is inevitable and justifiable. Indeed, unless the experience issues in outward behaviour, it is not experience at all. There cannot be a concave without a convex. But here too the principal kind of outward expression is a distinctive kind of behaviour. The Sermon on the Mount is our Lord's own account of this behaviour.

[1] See chap. ii. in *The Christian Experience*.

Our real difficulty, therefore, is not to describe it—for that has been done for us—but to decide how far behaviour may fall below this authoritative account of it, and yet be called ' Christian.' And, as already implied, I believe that the Church can point to a definite historical event, the life of Jesus, as the time of its birth, though here too there is a sense in which it may be said to have existed before that time. In a way the Old Testament tells a part of the story of the Christian society.

Wherever there is this Christian experience, evidenced by the inevitable and corresponding Christian behaviour, there, it seems to me, is the Christian Church. I do not think that anything can break the historic continuity of the Church except a breach in the continuity of this twofold thing, an inward Christian experience and the resultant Christian life. Schism, in the modern sense of the term, makes it difficult to retain the continuity, for, as will presently appear, outward continuity of government and ritual is of great value—but, while it makes it difficult, it does not make it impossible. As the historical continuity of the Italian nation survived a millennium of political division, so the historical continuity of the Christian Church has survived more than a millennium of schism. On the other hand, as the political disunity of Italy marred the full vigour of the Italian national life, so the schisms of the Christian Church have marred and do mar the vigour of the Church's life. There is much else to say here, of course, but it is time to turn more closely to our immediate subject.

The first and great *differentia* of the Church has been named already. At this point a second emerges. We have seen that the chief outward marks of the continuity of a nation are a common government, a common land, a common language, a common blood. None of these is a mark of the continuity of the Church. The Roman Christian, indeed, claims that a common government is

essential to the Church, but, so far as I understand, this
is not the Anglican opinion. Underlying the 'Lambeth
Appeal' of 1920, for instance, there lies the ideal of a
number of national churches, each in 'full communion'
with the others, but each autonomous. Again, many
Anglicans hold that there are three historic Churches, or
parts of the one Church—the Roman, the Greek, and the
Anglican. This opinion, too, seems to be incompatible
with unity of government. As for the other three bonds
or tokens of national unity, it is agreed that the Church
has neither land, nor language, nor blood in common.
*Just because it lacks such bonds, the directly symbolic is
for it of peculiar moment.* It follows that in the Church
symbols play a far greater part than in nations. No
other great society needs them so much.

But, while symbols reach their climax in the Church,
they are still symbols. In relation to historic continuity
their use is to serve as marks and means of the spiritual
fellowship that is the really continuative thing. It is
best here to omit the instance of the Sacraments, for it
will be found below that they have other uses than just
to mark continuity, and that I hold them to be obligatory
on the Christian Church, though not essential to it.
Further, they are not usually chosen as the outward sign
of historic continuity, though their unceasing repetition
through the centuries might be so taken. The Sacerdotalist points to the Apostolical Succession of bishops
when he seeks such a symbol. Indeed, for many
Sacerdotalists it is *the* God-selected and necessary symbol.
More still, they hold that by it 'grace' is conveyed from
one generation to another, and that without it there
would be no certain historical continuity at all.

I have spoken of some of the other questions that this
claim raises elsewhere. It would need an historical
investigation, pursuing the Christian generations one by
one, to examine whether this particular symbol has always

and everywhere been used, and we have seen that this is
not undertaken here. All that has been said above
against the claim that symbols are essential to the Church
could be said over again at this point. The pertinent
remark just here, however, is that it does not seem to me to
be possible to sustain the claim that this particular
symbol is essential to the historic continuity of the
Church. I allow at once that the unbroken succession of
bishops in the most ancient Sees is a very convenient and
impressive symbol of this continuity. Irenaeus was
justified in using it as such in the famous passage that has
roused so much controversy.[1] But it is not the only
possible symbol of continuity. For instance, appeal
might also be made to the historic Scriptures, used age by
age through the centuries ; or to the unbroken succession
of Sundays of Christian worship ; or to the continuous
acceptance of the historic Creeds. None of these is a
perfect token of continuity, but neither is a succession of
Ordinations by the laying on of bishops' hands. Canon
Lacey tells us that there is no proof of the universal use
of this symbol at any rate before the time of Cyprian.[2]
These tokens of the Church's continuity are like the
tokens of the continuity of a nation. The succession
of bishops, for instance, is parallel to the succession of
kings. Both are serviceable tokens of continuity, but
neither is essential to it. Just as France is still the same
nation, even though she has abandoned kings, so the
Church in Lutheran lands is still the same Church, even
though some branches of it have abandoned bishops.
The only essential to continuity is continuity in that
twofold thing, Christian experience and Christian ' conversation.'[3] Where these are, there is the Church. In

[1] The meaning of the passage is properly interpreted, so far as I can see, in
Headlam's *The Doctrine of the Church and Reunion*, pp. 124 ff.
[2] *The One Body and the One Spirit*, chap. iv.
[3] This concept of continuity, of course, is not a new one. It was held, for
instance, by Luther and other Reformers (Lindsay, *Luther and the German
Reformation*, pp. 223 f.).

the realm of Christian history, as elsewhere, the inward is primary, the outward derivative, and, among outward things, there is nothing essential except the Christian manner of life. As will appear in the next chapter, the only inevitable outward counterpart of the spiritual is the ethical, not the ritual. The last is useful ; it is so useful that it is folly to try to dispense with it ; but no particular ritual is essential to the continuity of the Church. The Non-Episcopal Churches are heirs of the Christianity of the past as well as the Episcopal Churches. The Methodist is historically one with Jesus of Nazareth as well as the Anglican.

It will perhaps make the Evangelical position clearer if I give some examples. Evangelicals hold that the historic continuity of the Church in the thirteenth century depended at least as much on the layman St. Francis as on the priest Innocent III ; in the fourteenth century more on the laywoman St. Catherine of Siena than either on the sanguinary Pope or the equally sanguinary Anti-Pope ; in the fifteenth century rather on the layman Thomas à Kempis than on the monster and priest Alexander VI, and in the sixteenth century more on Martin Luther than on Leo X. This is none the less true because St. Francis, St. Catherine, and Thomas à Kempis all held the Sacerdotal opinion. Where the Holy Spirit is welcomed into the hearts of men, there is the Christian experience ; this issues in Christian behaviour, which, in turn, strengthens Christian experience ; where these three are—the Spirit, the experience, and the behaviour—there is the Church. Where these three are, there too will be an appropriate Christian symbolism.[1] Inasmuch as the Church is an historical society, it is a great advantage if its symbols also be historical, as they

[1] I think that this will be so in some degree, even where an attempt is made to dispense with symbolism. As already seen (pp. 23 f.), the Society of Friends does not discard symbol in general ; I don't think that it has altogether succeeded in discarding religious symbol in particular.

then both express and feed the experience of a society whose life runs back to the First Advent and forward to the Second. But symbol cannot create experience ; and no particular symbol is essential to historic continuity.

The instances just given belong to a period about which there has been much controversy. There was a time when Protestant writers wrote as though in that period there were nothing good ; to-day others write as though there were nothing in it but good. No doubt in that period as in all others there was both good and bad. None the less, so far as I can see, at that time corruption was very rife in Christianity—and rife for a given reason. For the same reason it tends to be rife wherever the Sacerdotalist opinion prevails. I wish to be fair to Sacerdotalists, and I do not think that this kind of corruption is due to Sacerdotalism itself, but to an easy distortion of it. As I understand its exponents, they claim that, wherever there is Episcopal Ordination, there is ' grace,' whether the priest so ordained be and remain himself a Christian or not. They go on to say, however, that this ' grace ' is not available to any one, but only to those who sincerely seek to live the Christian life. Historically the opinion has widely and popularly prevailed that it is available for any one to whom the priest chooses to appoint it. Often this has meant ' to any one who pays for it.' I have in a previous chapter denied that the Sacerdotalist opinion can rightly be called magical. It seems to me that this historic perversion of it deserves to be called both ' magical ' and ' superstitious.' It seems to me, too, that it is a very easy and very disastrous perversion of the Sacerdotalist opinion, and one that through many centuries and peoples has worked havoc in the Church of Christ. Nor do I think that the perversion has perished. Is it not still rife in the larger part of Christendom ? If I may do so without impertinence, I would implore every devout Sacerdotalist to make it ever clearer and clearer that he repudiates this ancient and poisonous error. Historically it has proved terribly easy to pass from the assertion that the outward and symbolic is *an* essential of Christianity to the assertion that it is *the* essential. So far as I can judge, the prevalence of this last belief has been the chief curse of Christianity. It lies, for instance, behind all the abuses of the Mass, the Interdict, Indulgences, and the cult of Images. In all such abuses the root error is the error of the idolater—the belief that some outward thing opens or shuts the door to God. It will be noted that I use the word ' abuses,' for I do not here discuss whether these things have any use. But the abuse is fearfully easy. There is a magical or superstitious concept of Christian symbols. It is logically distinct from the Sacerdotal opinion, but whether they are historically separable remains still to be seen. Hitherto superstition has dogged Sacerdotalism as his shadow dogs a man.

III

THE ATTITUDE OF THE BIBLE TO RITUAL

A. INTRODUCTORY

THERE are very different opinions among Christians about
the nature and authority of the Bible, yet all agree that,
if the Bible gives definite teaching on any subject, its
teaching is important. Many count it, not only important, but authoritative. Consequently all those who have
discussed the Christian attitude to symbols have appealed
to its evidence. Two kinds of appeal, however, are
possible. Appeal may be made to the comparatively
small number of passages in the New Testament that
directly name the Sacraments of the Christian Ministry.
This appeal is valid. Yet there is a second kind of
appeal to Scripture, and to me it seems as valuable. At
the beginning of the Lecture it was pointed out that the
doctrines of the Sacraments and Ministry fall under a
wider question—the question of the relation of the
outward to the inward in all human life, or, at the least,
the question of the relation of the outward to the inward
in the part of life called religion and worship. Many
particular texts refer to this wider subject, but it is not
confined to them. On the contrary, it is one of the chief
subjects of the whole Bible. In this chapter an attempt
is made to trace the discussion of this subject historically
—that is, to show how it was dealt with period by period
in the history of Israel, how the final findings of the Old
Testament upon it are among the presuppositions of the

New Testament, and how they were applied by Our Lord and the Apostles to the problems of their own time. It seems to me that the ultimate attitude of the Bible to this wider subject is unmistakable. If this be so, it ought to be a weighty, if not a decisive, element in the debate about the meaning of the particular New Testament texts that refer to the Sacraments and Ministry. In other words, if the teaching of the Bible upon the broad question of the relation of the outward to the inward in religion be discovered, it is right to use that teaching as a criterion of judgement when particular texts are in question. The two kinds of appeal to the Bible are related, and they are related in this particular way—that the one is regulative of the other.

I make no apology for giving a large place here to the teaching of the Old Testament. It is agreed by all Christians that it has a right place in the Canon, and that it prepared the way for the New Testament. Or, to use a better phrase, it is agreed that, in the history of Israel, man was led to the discovery of certain religious truths which underlie Christianity. The most famous of these truths is summed in the phrase ' ethical monotheism.' There is no elaborate exposition or defence of this in the New Testament. It is simply assumed. Like the foundation of a building, it is unseen but essential. Without it there could be no New Testament. There are other such doctrines, too. To quote the greatest teacher of all, ' Salvation is of the Jews.' There were subjects on which the Old Testament reached a definite conclusion which is axiomatic for Jesus and the Apostles.

Of course, I am aware that some, who agree that there are such subjects, deny that the doctrine of symbols is one of them. They claim, I suppose, that here Jesus broke with the Hebrew past. It is a hazardous claim when the importance of the place given by the Old Testament to the wider question of the relation of the outward and inward is considered. This will, I hope, be clear when the discussion below has proceeded. Again, as will also appear below, it seems to me that on the wider subject the New Testament does clearly accept and use the Old Testament conclusions. If this be so, very cogent reasons indeed must be adduced to show that it makes exceptions, and I do not think that such reasons have been given. Rather, it seems to me that the teaching of the Old Testament about the relation of the outward to the inward in religion is normative for Christian thought.

B. The Old Testament

Before dealing with the Old Testament evidence, it is desirable to look more closely at the words ' outward ' and ' inward.' Sometimes it is assumed that this pair of words is parallel to the pair ' ritual ' and ' moral.' This is not so. The ' moral ' is itself both inward and outward. The inward temper that is religious, and that may be termed ' spiritual ' [1] implies and grows out of fellowship with God, and it shows itself, according to the Bible and to Christianity, both in ethical character and moral behaviour. [2] It also shows itself in the realm that is variously called ' ritual ' or ' ceremonial ' or ' Sacramental ' or ' Sacerdotal.'   To use the technical term, with a given religion there always goes a given *cultus*.   The inward temper or disposition of the religious man has two outward expressions—the moral, in which the religious temper shows itself primarily in behaviour towards other

---

[1] This word has been used earlier in its broadest sense—as synonymous with ' inward ' and ' psychical.' It is now used in its narrower and more accurate sense—as descriptive of experience that involves fellowship with God. Under this definition it is related to the psychical in much the same way as the Sacramental to the symbolic.

[2] For convenience I use the term ' ethical ' below for the inward quality and the term ' moral ' for its outward manifestation.

men, and the ritual, in which the religious temper expresses itself primarily in outward behaviour towards God. The word ' primarily' is inserted because in the ' moral' God is involved, and in the ' ritual' other men are involved, in each instance in a characteristic way. The spiritual, then, is purely inward ; the moral is both inward and outward ; the ritual is purely outward. It is the relation of the spiritual to the ritual that is now under investigation. This point is not unimportant, for it is not possible to examine the Old Testament attitude to *cultus* without referring to its attitude to that other outward thing— moral conduct. If the word ' worship' may be used in its narrower sense—of direct and conscious fellowship with God—one might say that we are here examining the relation of the spiritual and ritual to each other in worship.

A term is often wanted to include all the different material media of worship. The *cultus* of any given religion uses many such media. Some of the commonest are the altar, the image, the temple, sacrifices, a sacred book ; even the priest might be included. I venture to use the Greek word *sebasma*, with its plural, *sebasmata*, to denote the different items in a given *cultus*.

The subject of the place of the *cultus*, with its constituent *sebasmata*, in Old Testament religion, may be dealt with in four periods—the Patriarchal period ; the period from the Exodus to the coming of the Assyrian (i.e. from Moses to Amos) ; the period from Amos to the Exile (*c.* 750–586 B.C.) ; the Exilic and Post-Exilic period. For reasons that will appear below, these may be called ' The Patriarchal Period,' ' The Centuries of Hesitation,' ' The Period of the Prophets,' and ' The Period of the Priests.' Old Testament scholars differ about many details of the story, and especially about the place of images in the second period. But about the main lines of development there is no serious disagreement. Where it has been necessary below to take a side on such a question, I have

stated my own opinion, with an intimation that others
take different views, without entering into detailed
argument, as agreement on such points is not germane
to the present discussion. For the dates of the Old
Testament books I have followed such authorities as
Driver's *Introduction to the Old Testament*, and Hastings'
Dictionary of the Bible.

In the story of the Patriarchs the most obvious trait
is their relation to Jehovah.[1] This is the central
phenomenon ; all else is secondary. It is not possible
to say much more about its spiritual content than that
they did what Jehovah told them to do. The facts about
the outward *cultus* that they practised are few. There
are instances of the use of animal sacrifice and of altars.
In the story of Jacob, certain *sebasmata* of household
worship called ' teraphim ' are mentioned. Again, the
Patriarchs often worshipped at sacred spots, marked by a
stone, a tree, or a well. These were not the god that they
worshipped, but seem to be treated as a kind of guarantee
of His presence. At the same time, His worship is not
completely localized, for He is with the Patriarchs in
Ur and Egypt and Haran, as well as at the stone at Bethel,
the well at Beer-Sheba, and the tree at Mamre. Apart
from the doubtful instance of the ' teraphim,' there is no
example of the use of the image. It is a common opinion
that in the most ancient *cultus*, at any rate among Semitic
people, and even among all ' primitive ' tribes, the image
is not one of the earliest *sebasmata*. About the answer
to the immediate question before us—What was the
relation of the ritual to the spiritual ?—there is no clear
evidence, but it seems probable that no particular
sebasmata were counted essential to worship, though a
number were used.

In the period between Moses and Amos a larger number
of *sebasmata* occur. The distinctively priestly man, the

[1] I use this form as the current English name of the God of Israel.

so-called 'Levite,' appears ; but worship, including
sacrifice, might still be practised without him.[1] There
are a number of sacred places—as Shiloh, Bethel, Dan—
but it is impossible to say how many. It does not appear,
however, that it was thought impossible to meet with
Jehovah away from these places, for some stories tell
that Hebrews met with their God when away from the
sacred spots.[2] Animal sacrifices were used, and there
were three sacred seasons in each year, one or more in
each month, and one in each week—the Sabbath. But
there is no suggestion that worship was secluded to these
seasons. Other *sebasmata* are the ark, the ephod, the
teraphim, the pillar, the asherah or sacred pole, the
graven image, the molten image, the altar. Of these, the
ark was perhaps the most important, yet many Hebrews
worshipped without it. It was thought of as specially
helpful, but not as essential. This appears, for instance,
from David's desire to deposit it in his stronghold of
Jerusalem, on the one hand, and from Solomon's worship
at Gibeon, when the ark was in his capital, on the other.
The pillar seems to have been used at every shrine ; there
is no single mention of the asherah without condemnation.
This seems curious, and even unreasonable, to us at first,
for what difference could there be between the use of a
stone pillar and a wooden pole ? In practice, however,
there was a great difference. It seems almost certain that
at Canaanite shrines—and many places seem to have
been sacred both to the Hebrew and the Canaanite—the
asherah was associated with that immoral and impure
worship whose slime lies over almost all the popular
worship of Asia. Perhaps it was that the pole was early
carved into a woman's form. If so, then it led to
polytheism as well as to uncleanness. The altar was
in universal use, and, with it, both animal and other
sacrifices. In the earliest documents the 'molten image'

[1] e.g. Judges xvii.   [2] e.g. Judges xiii.

F

—i.e. a ' graven image ' covered with melted metal—was
forbidden to Israel. Was the graven image itself
permitted? About this scholars differ. The answer
would be clearer if it were certain what the ephod and
teraphim were. Three opinions may be distinguished.
Some hold that in the centuries in question all Israel
used images of Jehovah in worship, and saw no harm in it.
The most famous instances are the ' golden calves ' of
Jeroboam I at Bethel and Dan. A second opinion
declares that, while images of Jehovah were frequently
used, yet all knew that their use was forbidden by the
Law of Jehovah.[1] There would be a parallel to this, for
example, in the almost universal reverence paid to the
tombs of saints in Islam, against the explicit command of
the Koran. The third answer is, in effect, that throughout
this period there were two practices, and with them two
types of teaching, in Israel—some worshipping by means
of images, and some refusing so to do. This opinion is
perhaps the most reasonable, for, as seen above, it is
generally admitted that the image is not one of the most
primitive *sebasmata*, and, when later Hebrew writers
condemn image-worship, they sometimes seem to declare
that it was not original in Israel.[2] If this opinion be true,
it may prove that, generally speaking, image-worship was
practised in the North, while it was forbidden in Judah.
To return, however, to our main question, it is clear that,
in this period, there were many *sebasmata* in common use,
and that, whether they were counted essential to worship
or not, they were reckoned of value. When David was a
fugitive, for instance, he counted himself happy when
the priest Abiathar joined him with the ephod. Other
nations beside Israel followed the practices that have so
far been named. Yet Israel had a distinctive possession.
This is often briefly summed up in ' The Prophets.' Two

[1] This opinion would, of course, hold the field if it were proved that the
Second Commandment belongs to this period.
[2] e.g. Amos v. 25 ; Jer. vii. 21 f.

comments need to be added. Some of the phenomena of prophecy are found among other peoples—the prophetic frenzy, for instance—and the full development of the distinctive character of Hebrew prophecy did not occur till the next period. Second, something else was already beginning to be distinctive of Israel, as may be seen from the ' Book of the Covenant,' the first collection of Hebrew laws.[1] If this be examined, there is already good evidence of that connexion of morality with religion which was more and more to become the mark of Hebrew faith. In the stories of the earlier Prophets, too, this quality is already noticeable. The story of Nathan's rebuke of David for adultery, and of Elijah's rebuke of Ahab for the theft of Naboth's vineyard, are the most famous illustrations. Yet in the Book of the Covenant there are commands about *cultus* side by side with commands that require justice, mercy, and truth. Again there is no hint that the Prophets of this period rejected the *cultus*. On the other hand, Samuel offered sacrifices, and Elijah at Carmel ' repaired the altar of Jehovah that was broken down.' There were, therefore, already two outward elements in the religion of Jehovah—the moral and the ritual—and as yet no undoubtedly clear distinction is made between them.

With the next period, stretching from Amos to Jeremiah we reach the greatest era of Hebrew religion, and with it the threefold distinction already named—between the spiritual, the moral, and the ritual—becomes as clear as day. The first of these—the spiritual—is, of course, found wherever there is religion, but a thing may be in a man's experience long before he is fully aware of it, and still longer before he is able fully to describe and define it. In the Covenant between Abraham and Jehovah there was, of course, a spiritual fellowship, though perhaps Abraham would not have understood so abstract a term,

[1] Exod. xxi–xxiii.

nor was even fully conscious of the ' inwardness ' of his faith at all. For him religion was obedience ; his God told him to do something, and he did it. It is the modern psychologist who examines this phenomenon and discerns that it must have had an inward or spiritual side. The same is true of the period that followed the Patriarchal. We feel that to use the term spiritual of the religion of David, or even of Elijah, is somehow an anachronism. This is not because there was no inward fellowship with God in the religion of these ancient saints, but because in their time the introspective mood in men had not so far developed as to lead them to speak of ' inward ' and ' outward.' They had an experience that they did not examine at all in a psychological way. For them the word Covenant is a more correct description of religion than ' fellowship,' even though Covenant implies fellowship. With the great Prophets of the eighth and seventh centuries before Christ, however, all this is altered. I do not mean, of course, that they were psychologists in any scientific sense, but that, in their own way, they did clearly make the distinction between the inward and the outward in their fellowship with God. In other words, when their oracles are examined, there is clear consciousness of what we mean by ' spiritual.' It is impossible, for instance, to read the story of Isaiah's vision, or Jeremiah's prophecy of the Covenant of the Heart, without recognizing that these men knew what introspection means, that they were psychological without saying so, and that they had the concept that we call spiritual. Now the inward was not only an element in religion, but it was known as the higher and regulative element.

Similarly, it is quite clear that the Prophets of this time recognized that the outward in religion falls into two forms, the moral and the ritual, and that they insisted that the first of these is more important than the second. Many readers of their books would say that,

after the denunciation of apostasy, this is their chief
message. ' I desire mercy and not sacrifice,' cried Hosea
in the name of Jehovah[1]; ' Bring no more vain obla-
tions. . . . Cease to do evil, learn to do well,' demanded
Isaiah[2]; ' Take away the foreskin of your hearts,'
pleaded Jeremiah[3]; ' Will the Lord be pleased with
thousands of rams, or with ten thousands of rivers of
oil? ' asked Micah. ' . . . What doth the Lord require
of thee but to do justly and to love mercy and to walk
humbly with thy God? '[4] These are only a few of the
most familiar instances of an iterated and reiterated
message of these Prophets. They insist, until they have
beggared insistence, that, of the two outward results of
religion, the moral is far more important than the ritual.
They put our three phenomena in this order—first the
spiritual, then the moral, then the ritual. None can
read their books and deny this.

It is possible, however, to put several things in order of
importance—saying that the last are less important than
the first—and yet to claim that all of them, from the
first to the last, are essential. In the instance of religion,
for example, it is possible to hold that, while the spiritual
is fundamental to the moral, and while the moral is more
important than the ritual, yet all three are essential.
Here we approach closely to our present subject. What
do the Prophets say on this point?

There is no difference of opinion about the first two of
the series of three. All agree that the Prophets teach
that the spiritual is essential in religion, and, indeed,
fundamental; they also agree that the Prophets teach
that the spiritual cannot thrive, or, rather, cannot live
at all, unless it expresses itself in moral behaviour. But
what of its other outward expression? What of the ritual?

Here, again, we come upon a point of difference among
scholars. Some hold, on the basis of several great passages,

[1] Hos. vi. 6.   [2] Isa. i. 13, 16 f.   [3] Jer. iv. 4.   [4] Mic. vi. 7 f.

that the Prophets of this era rejected ritual altogether. If these passages be taken literally, this claim is proved. But it is the custom of preachers of all ages to concentrate attention upon the immediately practical and urgent part of the truth. Sometimes they leave other parts unspoken, or even seem to deny them. Probably no preachers have gone farther than the Prophets in this direction. Again, there are other passages in these very Prophets' books that assert or require the value of ritual. The same Hosea who declares, ' Thus saith the Lord, I desire mercy and not sacrifice,' depicts the loss of sacrifice, pillar, ephod, and teraphim as a curse.[1] If Isaiah cried, ' Hear the word of the Lord . . . I delight not in the blood of bullocks, or of lambs, or of he-goats,' it was in the Temple that he saw his first great vision, and its *sebasmata* gave the vision its form.[2] Jeremiah declared, indeed, ' Thus saith the Lord of Hosts . . . I commanded not your fathers in the day that I brought them out of the land of Egypt concerning burnt offerings or sacrifices,' yet he preached a very vigorous sermon in defence of the Sabbath.[3] It seems to me, therefore, that these Prophets rather enunciated the secondariness of ritual than demanded its abolition.

It is clear, however, that they demanded the abolition of certain *sebasmata*. Here two are the most prominent —the asherah and the image. The reasons for the denunciation of the first of these have already been suggested. As to the image, it is not easy to give logical and theoretical reasons for denouncing its use, as the history of iconoclasm in the Christian Church shows, but the Prophets were neither mere logicians nor mere theorists. Their denunciations built upon experience. Centuries of experience had shown that the use of images brought three evils. First, when images were used, it was easy to pass from the worship of Jehovah only to

[1] Hos. vi. 6, iii. 4.   [2] Isa. i. 10 f. ; vi. 1 ff.   [3] Jer. vii. 21 f., xvii. 19 ff.

the worship of many gods, for the multitude of images easily led to the multiplication of divinities. Next, when images were used, some were female images, and stood for goddesses, and, as soon as sex is admitted in gods, impurity in worship accompanies polytheism. Thirdly, in experience the use of images readily led to superstition, or, to employ the term in its general and not in its strictly scientific sense, to the magical. That is, the idea followed that some religious benefit could be got through the image, even if there were no spiritual desire, or even religious temper, in the worshipper. For these three reasons the Prophets banned the image. The experience of Christian centuries has shown that, while the second evil does not accompany the use of images in Christian worship, the other two still cleave to it. Polytheism, indeed, does not recur in name, but the cult of Mary and the saints has often approached it. The risk of the superstitious or magical use of images needs no argument. In the Prophets' treatment of these *sebasmata* there is an ' object lesson ' for all later ages. Given media of worship are to be used or rejected, not merely or chiefly for logical or theoretical reasons, but on practical grounds. A given rite is to be approved if it helps men to be spiritual ; it is to be rejected if it hinders rather than helps. Of course, much else would need to be said if the whole subject of the Christian use of ikon and image were under discussion. I am only suggesting that in the discussion the witness of these Prophets should not be overlooked. I ought perhaps to add that the Book of Deuteronomy, which probably belongs, in its present form, to this period, says the same things as the Prophets about the use of images. About the lawfulness of ritual, on the other hand, its evidence, unlike that of the Prophets, is undisputed. It does, of course, recognize the lawfulness and the value of ritual in the worship of Jehovah.

For the present investigation another point, however, is more pertinent. While scholars differ whether the great Prophets of the later monarchy demanded the abolition of ritual or not, there is no difference among them about the answer to another question : Did these Prophets count ritual essential to religion ? All agree that they did not. For them the spiritual and the moral were essential, but the ritual fell among secondary and non-essential things. And, in particular, they taught that no one ritual use or ritual emblem or *sebasma* was essential. The outstanding instance is the great *sebasma* called the Temple. Originally built to shelter the ark, it gradually superseded this as the chief *sebasma* of Israel. It was a thing that all could see, while the ark became a hidden treasure. Moreover, in the crisis of Sennacherib's invasion the Temple, alone of all the shrines of Jehovah, proved invulnerable. Isaiah's cry, ' This shrine shall not fall,' uttered again and again when the capture of the last of Israel's cities seemed only a question of days, or even hours, proved true. The Temple did not fall. In the ensuing century an almost inevitable result ensued. The people, exultant with the deliverance from Sennacherib, cried, ' The Temple cannot be taken ; Jehovah will not let it fall.' And by the days of Jeremiah they had silently added a significant clause. In effect, they said, ' Jehovah will not let the Temple fall, whatever we do, however hardily we sin.' It was this situation that Jeremiah had to face. His courage was never more evident than when he ' stood in the gate of the house of Jehovah ' and cried, ' Trust ye not in lying words, saying, The Temple of the Lord, the Temple of the Lord, The Temple of the Lord, is this ! . . . I will do unto the house which is called by My name, wherein ye trust, and unto the place which I gave to you and to your fathers, as I have done to Shiloh.' [1]   True to the spirit of Isaiah,

[1] Jer. vii. 2, 4, 14.

Jeremiah literally contradicted him. ' This Temple shall not fall,' his great predecessor had said ; ' This Temple shall fall,' said he. Yet Jeremiah did not go on to say that religion would perish with the Temple. Rather, he assumed that true religion could now only survive and develop in exile. And here, too, he proved right. In the instance of the greatest *sebasma* of Israel, Jeremiah protested that no particular ritual is essential to religion. To revert to the word of an earlier chapter, he declared that the symbolic is secondary and variable ; it is the spiritual and the moral that are essential. The ' new covenant,' which he proclaimed in his deepest and most characteristic passage, had nothing ' objective '—to misuse the word in the way that some do—about it at all. It was ' merely subjective ' ; it was a law written in the heart.[1]

The last of the Old Testament periods distinguished above begins with Ezekiel, and, at least for the present subject, to understand him is to understand it. In one half of his book he is a disciple of Jeremiah, though by no means a mere echo of that great teacher. Ezekiel insists on the need for a spiritual reformation of Israel. He practically uses the very word, for he cries out for, and promises, a new ' spirit ' in Israel. Nor does he lack denunciations of the use of asherah and image. He insists, again, upon the need for morality in the worshipper of Jehovah. But he differs markedly from his prophetic predecessors about ritual. As has been seen, they make so little of it that it is doubtful whether they find any place for it in religion at all. There is no such doubt about Ezekiel. The latter part of his book is a great description of a restored Temple. It is true that sometimes his vision soars into the impracticable, yet there is as little doubt that in the main it is meant to be a description of a real Temple. The description is, indeed,

---

[1] Jer. xxxi. 31 ff.

both of an actual and a symbolic sanctuary. Ezekiel has
the right concept of ritual ; it is to be symbolic of the
spiritual. It is not necessary to show this in detail. In
Ezekiel the priest and prophet blend. He gives a large
place alike to the spiritual, the moral, and the ritual.
But he has them in the right relation. The first is
primary ; the second is its necessary expression and
complement ; the third is the expression and the hand-
maid of the other two. It is probable that Ezekiel never
asked himself the question, ' Is any of this ritual—is the
very Temple itself, on whose description I have spent all
the powers of an opulent and loving imagination—
essential to the worship of Jehovah ? ' It was enough for
him that it would express the unity of Israel's future
with its past, would symbolize the reverences of a true
worship, would feed the experience that it expressed. If,
however, he had asked himself the question, ' Is it, after
all, essential ? Cannot there be the true spiritual worship
of Jehovah without it ? '—only one answer would have
been possible. For there were faithful worshippers of
Jehovah in the very Exile that he shared, and their
worship was real. He himself was the minister of such a
group of such people beside the Chebar. If sacrifice or
altar or ark or temple had been essential to the worship of
Jehovah, that worship would, of course, have perished
when Israel went into exile, for in exile they had none of
these things. With Ezekiel, then, we reach the same
conclusion as we reached by psychological scrutiny in an
earlier chapter—that ritual is valuable when it is Sacramental, that is, when it expresses and feeds the inward
and spiritual ; none the less, no particular ritual is
essential.

It is interesting to notice how this attitude recurs in
other Prophets of the period, for here they contrast
strongly with their great predecessors. Haggai and
Zechariah prophesied in order to promote the rebuilding

of the very Temple whose destruction Jeremiah had predicted. Again, the chief burden of Malachi is the need for a right use of ritual. In his days it was undervalued and neglected. It was no longer eagerly pursued as a substitute for righteousness, but it had become a mere ' weariness ' through formalism.[1] This Prophet, therefore, does not cry out upon its uselessness, but demands that it shall be given its right place in life. What he denounces is not ritual, but formalism. In the phraseology used above, he demands that ritual shall not be mechanical, but symbolic. He is a Sacramentalist. One more Prophet may be mentioned—the nameless man whom we call Deutero-Isaiah. At first sight it seems as if there were no place for ritual in his thought. Surely, to take the greatest example, in the Fifty-Third Chapter he speaks of a spiritual experience, and of that only. It is true that in the forefront of this deep teacher's message the spiritual stands by itself. For him it is indeed *the* thing that makes true religion. Yet away in the background there is something else. He preaches a Return. Why? Why should not Israel remain in the far places of the earth, and worship its God there? There is a Sacramental land far away, and in it there is a peculiarly Sacramental place, and his heart yearns for both. The reticence of this writer, no less than the many words of Ezekiel, bears witness at once to the secondariness and the value of the outward in religion. In his thought the outward and the inward has each its right place. He preaches and sings of the spiritual, and he knows that the Sacramental will ensue.

There is another kind of document, however, that belongs to the Exilic and Post-Exilic Period. Scholars call it ' the Priestly Code,' and its most characteristic part is the Book of Leviticus. It is largely a description of the ritual of the Second Temple. There are parts of it that

[1] Mal. i. 13.

some Evangelicals find it hard to deal with. They
distinguish sharply between the Prophet and the Priest,
claiming the former for themselves and leaving the latter
to the Sacerdotalist. They find their task easy in the
period preceding the Exile, for almost every Prophet,
from Amos to Jeremiah, denounces the Priest. Their
difficulties begin with Ezekiel, and they often leave that
Priest-Prophet severely alone. Then comes Leviticus !
They say, indeed, that its ritual was a 'shadow'
of the 'better things to come,' but they often forget
that such a 'shadow' has value. Yet, on the other
hand, the book is not altogether to the hand of the
Sacerdotalist. When he begins to examine it, he finds
it intractable, too—so much so, indeed, that some
Sacerdotalists roundly declare that there is nothing
'Sacramental' in the Old Testament at all. Is there no
third way ?

First, it is to be remembered that the Priestly Code
does find a place for the moral. In the so-called Code of
Holiness, in particular,[1] there is much that is ethical,
and obedience to ethical demands is claimed in the name
of the 'holiness' of Jehovah. In other words, in this
book 'holiness' is not merely ceremonial. It uses the
word 'holy' indifferently, as it is still used in English
to-day,[2] both of the moral and the ritual. One example
of ethical teaching will suffice. It is in this Code that
the great ethical command, 'Thou shalt love thy neighbour as thyself,' first occurs.[3] But, further, it is to be
remembered that the parts of the Code that give themselves to the description of ritual do not seek to do any
more than this. A 'manual for celebrants' is not
expected to contain a *rationale* of the ceremonies it
describes. It does not at all follow that they have no

[1] Lev. xvii.–xxvi.

[2] e.g. we speak both of 'a holy man' and 'a holy day.' The link, of course,
is the old one—both are devoted to God.

[3] Lev. xix. 18.

spiritual meaning. For instance, it is true that the Sixteenth Chapter of Leviticus does no more than describe the proper ritual of the Day of Atonement ; it does not pretend to do more. But if a man will read until he can see—if he will follow the High-Priest, white-robed in penitence for this one occasion, into the Holy of Holies ' with the blood,' while the people wait without—if he will watch the ' scapegoat ' wander, sin-laden, into the wilderness—if he will rejoice with Israel as the High-Priest dons again the robes of his splendour and begins again the daily sacrifice that marked the unity of Israel with its Lord—if he will do these things, he will find it very difficult to dismiss the ' whole thing ' as ' mere ritual.' It is one of the finest examples in all history of the Sacramental use of the outward.

Yet a challenge may fall : ' What proof is there that any Israelite had any such spiritual experience even on that great Day ? ' The answer is ready : The Book of Psalms. For it is becoming clearer and clearer that the Psalter was ' the hymn-book ' of the Second Temple. [1] Like other hymn-books, it may, of course, contain many songs that are much older than the collection, but the collection as we now have it seems certainly to have been made at this time, and to have been made for use in the Temple. No doubt it also had other uses ; no doubt ultimately it was used in Synagogues, too ; but its primary purpose was for the worship of Jehovah in the Temple at Jerusalem. Not a few of the Psalms, indeed, seem to have been composed expressly for Temple-worship. If, therefore, tokens of the religious temper of Post-Exilic Judaism are sought, it is necessary to take the Priestly Code and the Book of Psalms together. What ensues ? There is no Old Testament book where the

---

[1] See, for instance, two recent books—A. C. Welch, *The Psalter in Life, Worship, and History*, and *The Psalmists* (edited by D. C. Simpson).

spiritual nature of true religion is more clearly enunciated
than in the Book of Psalms.   Otherwise it would not have
been favourite with Christian saints for a pair of millenniums.   It could not be the hymn-book of men who were
mere ceremonialists.   If the two books are taken together,
we reach once more the old conclusion—that in the worship
of Jehovah there was a place both for the spiritual, the
moral, and the ritual, but that these three properly bore
a given relation to each other.   To sing the Psalms was
to declare that Jehovah is Himself spiritual, and that a
spiritual worship is alone His delight.   It was to confess,
too, that only one with ' clean hands '—only a man who
strove to do right by his neighbour—could be a truly
spiritual man.   And there was a third assertion.   It can
be found in the Psalter itself.   There is a great instance
in the Fifty-First Psalm.   It has often been claimed that
its last two verses are a later ritualistic addition to it.   Is
this so certain ?   Even if they were added, surely they
were added by a man who understood the right relation
of the inward and the outward.   He knew what spiritual
religion was.   Had he not said, ' Against Thee, Thee only,
have I sinned,' and ' Hide Thy face from my sins,' and
' Create in me a clean heart, O God,' and ' The sacrifices
of God are a broken spirit ' ?   It does not follow at all
that he had no use for ritual.   He knew that there is a
place for the Sacramental in worship, if only it is subordinate to the spiritual.   He boldly claims that this is
so in the will of God.   His beloved city and its beloved
Temple do serve his spiritual need.   Jehovah, he declares,
does delight in ' bullocks upon the altar,' if only they be
' the sacrifices of righteousness.'   So the Old Testament
closes with the inward and the outward—the spiritual,
the moral, the ritual—in their right places.   God
wills the third, as well as the first and the second, if
only it be their servant and not their master or
substitute.   It is the spiritual that validates the ritual,

not the ritual that guarantees the spiritual. This is the final finding of the Old Testament.[1] Israel was a Sacramental Society.

C. The New Testament

All those who accept the Old Testament as part of their Bible believe that the New Testament inherits much of its teaching. Sometimes it develops that teaching, bringing it to its climax in Christ, but sometimes it just takes the Old Testament teaching for granted. It may do so silently, or it may mention the teaching incidentally. It will make the last distinction clear if I give an example of each method.

One of the chief heirlooms of the Old Testament is monotheism, the belief that there is but one God. This tenet is assumed throughout the New Testament. It is one of the truths that are counted too obvious to argue, too obvious even to assert. Another of the Old Testament truths that the New Testament inherits is the belief that idolatry is sin. There is no argument to prove this, for it too can be taken for granted. But, as it happened, there was need to mention it incidentally in such passages as the First Chapter of Romans.[2] The New Testament pre-supposes many of the teachings of the Old, sometimes silently, sometimes with incidental mention.

But further, the New Testament repudiates certain Old Testament beliefs. For instance, it denies the

[1] I mean, of course, that this is the teaching of the book, and not that every Israelite knew and practised the teaching. There would be many Jews, again, who had never thought out the distinction between the moral and ritual, just as there are many Christians to-day who have not done so. There are multitudes, for instance, who have not realized that there is ritual in the Decalogue, or that they use ' holy ' in two ways (see footnote on p. 92). It seems likely that the authors of such ' Priestly ' documents as Leviticus did not clearly make this distinction, for the moral and ritual intermingle indiscriminately in their writings. This is so in all the codes of Hebrew law.

[2] Rom. i. 23.

necessity for circumcision or for the continuance of the Jewish sacrifices. It does not do this, however, silently or incidentally. Before these things could be abandoned, the Epistles to the Romans and the Hebrews needed to be written. It is easy to see why this is so. The first Christians were Jews ; even when Christianity spread among the Gentiles, its apostles were Jews. For all the first Christian churches the Old Testament was a Bible. There is no need to stay to prove this. It is written large over the whole New Testament. While, therefore, it could be taken for granted that the teaching of the Old Testament was true, without argument, there was need for much discussion before any of its doctrines were abandoned. It could not simply be taken for granted that they were untrue.

In the previous section of this chapter we have seen that under the leadership of the Prophets the Old Testament reached a certain conclusion about ritual. It made the spiritual fundamental in religion, and it claimed that where there is the spiritual, there inevitably there will be the moral, but it denied that any particular ritual observance is essential to religion, though it allowed finally that ritual might be useful and therefore justifiable. Does the New Testament accept or repudiate this doctrine ?

The Sacramental school of interpreters, as I cannot but call them, holds that here the New Testament accepts Old Testament teaching. The Sacerdotalist school holds that the New Testament repudiates it, for they claim that the New Testament teaches that a given ritual is essential to Christianity. Which school is right ? The discussion has often centred in the exegesis of a few important passages—the passages, I mean, of course, that refer to Baptism and the Lord's Supper and the Laying On of Hands. These are discussed elsewhere in the Lecture. But it seems to me that the New Testament, like the Old, takes a general attitude to the question of ritual, and that this attitude bears upon the exposition of those particular passages. Indeed, if there were alternative expositions for a given passage, the one being in itself as likely as the other, I should maintain that this general attitude would be decisive for the meaning of the passage.

In the teaching of our Lord Himself, as recorded in the Synoptic Gospels, it seems plain that He gave the same place respectively to the spiritual, the moral, and the ritual that we have found to be final for the Old Testament. All agree, of course, that He made the spiritual primary. His great doctrine of the Fatherhood of God means that God longs for the fellowship of man, and that man's ' chief end ' is to ' enjoy ' fellowship with God—and this is just the ultimate account of what ' spiritual ' means. Again, all agree that Jesus taught that the spiritual will inevitably show itself in the moral. He gave a new depth and range to the ethical and moral —as the Sermon on the Mount, for instance, shows—but He taught that it was the ' fruit ' of the spiritual. Do not vines yield ' grapes,' and fig-trees ' figs ' ? What did He teach about the ritual? So far as the Jewish ritual is concerned, He repeated the teaching of the Prophets[1] and denied that it has intrinsic value. On the other hand, it was ' His custom ' to worship in the Synagogue, and, when He cleansed the Temple court, He seems to me to have vindicated the place of ritual in worship. Again, by submitting to the baptism of John, He acknowledged that there is a place for ritual in religion. So far as I can understand, the act at once expressed an experience that had been growing within Him for thirty years, and nourished that experience. In other words, Jesus used ritual whenever it served its proper purpose. Again, I hold that Jesus adopted the custom of Baptism from John, and instituted the Sacrament of the Lord's

[1] e.g. Matt. ix. 13, xii. 7, xxiii. 18 ff. ; Mark xii. 33.

G

Supper Himself, because He recognized the high value
of ritual in religion.   Both uses expressed, and in expressing nourished, the spiritual experience of His disciples.
Alike in His treatment of the ritual of the Old Testament
and in His initiation of ritual for the society or Church
that He founded, Jesus seems to me to have taken the
attitude that I have called ' final ' for the Old Testament.
And in so doing He related the spiritual, the moral, and
the ritual in the perfect way.

It is claimed, of course, that in the Fourth Gospel our
Lord declares that there is something ritual that is
essential to His Church, or at the least that He there
tells us that something ritual is the only sure guarantee
of the spiritual.   This claim depends upon two passages,
one in the Third Chapter and one in the Sixth, which I
discuss elsewhere.   It will be allowed by all that in the
Fourth Gospel the spiritual, exactly in the sense defined
above, is made primary.   There is little mention of the
moral—the reason being that the writer could assume,
when he wrote, that all Christians knew that this would
ensue inevitably on the spiritual.   In his First Epistle
the writer says this with his own peerless kind of sim-
plicity.[1]   About ritual he says little, except in the passages
in dispute.   To me it is wellnigh incredible that such a
writer should make ritual causative or essential to the
spiritual.   I am not sure that his omission of the story
of the institution of the Eucharist does not imply that
he counted even its ritual secondary.[2]   He gives himself
in his greatest Chapters[3] to expound and emphasize its
spiritual meaning.   I am now, however, speaking of the
atmosphere of his thought, and atmosphere has to be
' sensed ' rather than described.   I have no right to
demand that others shall ' sense ' it as I do.

[1] e.g. 1 John i 6, iv. 20.
[2] It may be that in Chaps. i.–xi. he omits, for the most part, what was
already well known, but from Palm Sunday onwards this is not his method.
[3] xiii.–xvii.

It is otherwise, I think, with the Epistles of Paul and the Epistle to the Hebrews. Before I can make my meaning clear, we must recall the environment in which they were written.

In the period between the Old Testament and the New, there had been a subtle change in opinion about the relation of the three elements in religion, the spiritual, the moral, and the ritual. I have already suggested that, while the three were clearly distinguished by the great Prophets and the great Psalmists, the difference between the moral and the ritual is not plainly made in the writings of the 'Priestly' school.[1] In the period between the Testaments the opinion gradually came to be prevalent that *both* the moral and the ritual were the necessary complement of the spiritual. To give an illustration, it came to be believed that every true worshipper of God must not only keep the commandment against murder but be circumcised. Another result followed. The ritual being now put on a level with the moral, the latter came to be interpreted, like the former, in a wholly outward way. The result was Pharisaism. It emphasized the outward until it tended to forget the inward—or, at the least, it assumed that where there was the outward, there was the inward too. We know the result. There grew up various kinds of Pharisaism. One kind was hypocritical. In it the spiritual was lost altogether. Our Lord gibbeted it in words that none can forget. There was, however, another kind of Pharisaism. Its best example is Saul of Tarsus. No one suggests that in the days before his conversion Saul was a hypocrite. The Seventh of Romans contradicts that. In it Paul tells us that he knew that there was a spiritual, and he craved to win it. He tried to win it by plying the outward both in its moral and its ritual fashions, and he tried in vain. He discovered at last, to use homely phrases,

[1] See footnote on p. 95.

that he was ' putting the cart before the horse ' or
' beginning at the wrong end.' In and through fellowship
with Christ, Paul found the spiritual—and lo ! it issued
in the ethical and moral. The latter now was perfected
both on its inward and outward sides. What about the
ritual ? Did Paul, having discovered that even the moral,
so long as it is outward, will not produce the spiritual, and
is not even a sure guarantee of its presence, go on to
believe that a new ritual could produce it or was its sure
guarantee ? Was his great discovery merely that he had
been using the wrong kind of ritual ? If so, the Eighth
of Romans ought to be a great exposition of Baptism
as the necessary means of the Christian experience of
salvation. It will not do to say that he took this for
granted, as the common belief among Christians. Could he
not have taken the experience that he does describe in the
great Chapter also for granted ? The question is what
conclusion his argument requires. He is arguing
specifically about the place of the outward in religion,
and, if he thought that anything outward was essential,
he ought to have said so. He did think that something
outward was essential, and he said so. But this outward
thing was the moral, [1] not the ritual. He does not here
mention the last at all.

I have taken this great example, but, of course, it is only
an example. In the Epistle to the Galatians, for instance,
it seems to me that, on the Sacerdotalist showing, such
a text as ' Neither is circumcision anything, nor uncircumcision, but a new creature,' [2] has the wrong conclusion.
Paul declares that nothing ritual is essential. A Sacerdotalist would have said, ' Neither is circumcision anything, nor uncircumcision, but baptism.' I have discussed elsewhere the passages where Paul refers to the
Sacraments. They seem to me to prove that he found a
place for ritual in the new faith—that he valued it in its

[1] Ver. 12.   [2] Gal. vi. 15.

right place.   In other words, he gave a Christian application to the final teaching of the Old Testament—first the
spiritual, then the moral, then the ritual.   He does not
repudiate the final Hebrew conviction about the last,
but takes it for granted.

The general attitude of the New Testament to the place
of ritual in religion is clearest of all in the Epistle to the
Hebrews.   Its immediate purpose may be recalled.   As
the struggle between the Jew and the Roman drew to
one of its recurrent climaxes, the Christian Jew found
himself in a hard place.   He longed to remain true to the
church of his fathers, yet his new Master, Jesus, had left
clear directions that his followers were to take no part
in any armed conflict between the two races.[1]   If he
refused to join the Jewish rebels, he would be dubbed
traitor ; if he joined them, he would be false to his Lord.
What was he to do ?   Further, to any one with a seeing
eye, it seemed more and more certain that Rome would
prevail in the struggle, and would she not then destroy
the Temple that was the very citadel of her foe ?   It may
even have been that the Temple was falling as the Epistle
was written.   What was a Christian Jew to believe about
this old, lost ritual, to which he, like his fathers, had
thought that the worship of the true God was wedded ?
We know the courage and the insight of the man who
wrote the Epistle.   He took as his principal example the
greatest instance of Hebrew ritual, the Day of Atonement,
and he showed that in Jesus the Christian has the sub-
stance of which that was the shadow.   He said, in effect,
that it was not the ritual that was essential to worship,
but the spiritual things for which it stood ; and he added
that these spiritual things are perfected once for all in
Christ.   In so saying, he transferred certain details of
the ritual to the skies.   He declared that we have a
High-Priest, of a nobler type than Aaron's—for which he

[1] Mark xiii. 14 ff.

found an Old Testament analogue in Melchizedek—that He is at once Victim and Priest, that He has passed within a heavenly Holy of Holies, and that there He offers a worthier blood than that of ' bulls and goats,' so putting away sin and restoring man to the high fellowship of God. All this is clearly symbolic. Jesus does not offer actual blood in the skies at any actual shrine. The ritual is taken throughout as typical or symbolic of the spiritual. Of the Old Testament ritual it is one of the writer's burdens to declare that it is not essential to the worship and fellowship of God, however ancient it may be and however many generations of devout men have found it to help their worship. The writer says, in fact, of the Hebrew ritual, what Paul says in another relation, ' The things that are seen are temporary, but the things that are unseen are eternal.'

But surely, on the Sacerdotalist opinion, something is lacking. If this man believed that there was a ritual that was essential to the new faith—even as the old ritual had been supposed essential to the old faith— he would go on to say so. Sacerdotalist writers, when they expound this Epistle, do go on to say so. They explain that, while the great High-Priest offers His blood in the heavens, other priests offer a corresponding sacrifice on earth. With their convictions they are right in making this addition. But the writer did not make it. Why ? It would have been exactly pertinent to his argument, if he had held the opinion in question. He would have said, ' Do not grieve because you have lost the old ritual ; we Christians have a new and better ritual—better because it can do what the old ritual could not do. Rejoice in it.' Such a conclusion would have comforted his readers exceedingly—if it were true—for human nature leans hard on the outward, as the whole history of religion shows. But the writer speaks, instead, of ' the mediator of a better covenant,' quoting Jeremiah's famous oracle of the primacy of the spiritual.[1] Considered with its original context, it is perhaps the least appropriate quotation in the whole Old Testament for the purposes of a Sacerdotalist. Again, there is general agreement that the writer's argument ends in the middle of Chapter Ten (ver. 18). It runs, ' There is no more offering for sin.' Could any one who believed that in the Eucharist there is a constant repetition of Christ's sacrifice, have left the sentence so ? This writer, like St. Paul, goes on to refer to something outward, but, again like St. Paul, it is to the moral he refers[2] not the ritual. At the point where the ritual must inevitably have been mentioned, if the writer had held it to be essential, it is not even named. In the Epistle to the Hebrews the old argument of the Prophets that ritual has no intrinsic value reaches its Christian climax. Or, to put the point in another way, the Sacerdotalist holds that in Christianity two things, the one heavenly and the other earthly, have fulfilled, surpassed, and superseded the Jewish ritual ; the Evangelical holds that one thing only, the heavenly Priesthood of Christ, does this. Which does the writer of this Epistle say ?

To sum up, there are tenets of the Old Testament that the gospel superseded. Paul argues this for Circumcision, and the writer to the Hebrews for Sacrifice. But, where there is no such argument, the general assumption of the New Testament is that the teaching of the Old Testament is still valid. Otherwise the Old Testament would not be part of the Bible. It is agreed that this is true of many Old Testament doctrines. One of its chief doctrines, a doctrine won through the agony of the great Prophets, is the doctrine that in religion the spiritual and not the ritual is essential. It is asserted by some, and denied by others, that in a few passages the New Testament makes the observance of a given ritual essential

---

[1] Jer. xxxi. 31 ff.   [2] Verses 19–31.

to Christianity.   It seems to me that the general attitude
of the New Testament, and indeed of the whole Bible,
to ritual, should carry great weight when these few
passages are examined.   And the general attitude of the
Bible to ritual seems to me beyond dispute.

IV

THE SACRAMENT OF BAPTISM

In the light of the discussions of the last two chapters
we may now consider more closely the two Sacraments
of Baptism and the Lord's Supper. This chapter, in the
main, deals with the first, and the next chapter with the
second. There are, however, certain truths that obtain
for both, and it is convenient to state these first. They
are, therefore, examined in the first section of this chapter.
There follow discussions of Baptism as it obtained in
New Testament times, and of the practice of Infant
Baptism.

A. SOME MARKS OF THE TWO SACRAMENTS

As already stated, I am among those who believe
that our Lord Himself taught His disciples to use the
Sacrament of Baptism and instituted the Sacrament of
the Lord's Supper. Here there is no difference of opinion
between such Evangelicals as myself and representative
Sacerdotalists. It follows that for me they are unique,
for I do not think that there is good evidence, or, indeed,
any evidence at all, that our Lord Himself authorized
and appointed anything else in the ritual of His Church.

It follows, also, that these two Sacraments are
obligatory upon Christians in a way that no other rite
can be. I have distinguished the words ' essential ' and
' obligatory ' above, and we shall need later to return

to the distinction.   But to say that the ' essential ' and
the ' obligatory ' are not the same does not mean that
obligatory observances are unimportant.   Of course,
there are different degrees of obligation.   They range
from the slight obligation that men feel to address a
mayor as ' Your Worship ' or to begin a letter with
' Sir ' or ' Dear Sir,' to the obligation to die for one's
country or home.   It may be said that the latter example
passes outside the realm of symbols, and this is true ;
yet even within that realm there is great variety in
obligation.   It ranges from the obligation to say ' Sir '
when addressing some one of an ill-defined set of people
to the obligation to give and take a ring in pledge of
marriage.   For the Christian who believes that the two
Sacraments have the authority of Christ, they are
obligatory as nothing else in the realm of the symbolic,
or even the Sacramental, can be.   Our Lord's authority
is final.   This is one of the things that can be very briefly
said ; and sometimes a reader is tempted to assume, a
little unthinkingly, that the things that fill most pages
in a book are always the most important.   Yet they
may fill space, not because they are important, but
because they are obscure or controversial.   The authority
of our Lord is neither.   The brevity of its mention
marks its obviousness, not its insignificance.   So far as
my own experience goes, the neglect of the Sacrament of
Baptism by Christians who believe that our Lord commanded it is very rare.   The common error here is not
neglecting the rite, but forgetfulness of its meaning.
How often parents bring their children to Baptism and
quickly forget its vows !   On the other hand, the
Sacrament of the Lord's Supper, as it often recurs, is
often neglected.   There is no excuse for such neglect.

The comparatively infrequent use of the Eucharist,
however, may not be synonymous with neglect.   It was
seen above that some people use a symbol more often

with the deepening of the experience that it expresses and feeds, while others use it less often.[1] This phenomenon has its highest instance here. There are saints who desire daily ' Communion ' because they are saints. John Wesley seems to have so desired it. There are saints, too, who do not dare to join in the Supper of their Lord without long examination and preparation. Few people can find time for this daily, or even weekly. Among the old Presbyterians the Sacrament only fell twice in the year, yet these were often such seasons of heart-searching and intimacy with Christ that they enriched the soul for the whole year. No rule applies to all Christians here. But what shall we say of the man who believes that his Lord gave him this commandment, and either neglects to follow it at all, or follows it as mere form ? Life teems with obligatory symbols ; here they reach their climax.

The two Sacraments are unique in another way. The one is the symbol of entrance into a certain society, the other of continuance in it. The society is the Church. I have already said something about the meaning that I give to this word. In the Church the society as a whole, and each of its members for himself, seeks willing and conscious fellowship with Christ. In considering the two Sacraments, therefore, three parties are involved— Christ, the Church, the individual Christian. For me the two last are related to each other because they are both related to Christ. The primary relation, both of the Christian and the Church, is to Him. They are in fellowship with each other because they are both in fellowship with Him. Of course, there is much more to be said of these relationships. Of course, too, there are controversies about them. But these lie a little outside the present purpose, and it is sufficient if I have made my own belief clear. The second unique fact about the two

[1] See pp. 30 ff.

Sacraments follows. They express and nourish a fellow-ship both of the Christian and the Church *with the Christ*. They are symbols of the New Covenant between the new mankind and its Head. This is not true of the other five rites that some call Sacraments. I do not mean that Christ has nothing to do with these. He has—or ought to have—much to do with Ordination, and Confirmation, and Marriage. I have no doubt that many who use the other two 'Sacraments'—Penance and Unction—often find that He uses these as means of blessing too. All these, therefore, as well as many other Christian rites, may be called 'Sacramental' in the second of the two senses distinguished above, as well as in the first. But there is a third and highest sense, applicable only to Baptism and the Lord's Supper. Not only were these appointed by our Lord Himself; they are 'signs and seals' of the fellowship that binds Him to 'believers'; and there are no other such 'signs and seals.' To use the Old Testament word, these two are symbols of the Covenant that is between God and man 'in Christ Jesus.'

It may already have been noticed that, among the symbols of human life in general, symbols of fellowship or of covenant hold a pre-eminent place. To use the word 'respectable' for once in its true sense, among all respectable people there is a kind of fellowship that is expressed by the hand-shake. This seems unimportant, until it is refused ! Or again, there is no need to recall the contumely that lay upon the head of a statesman who spoke of a treaty between nations as a 'scrap of paper.' He will be known for ever in history as the statesman who broke covenant. Once more, the example of the marriage 'lines' and the marriage ring suggest themselves. What do we think of any who make light of these ? Symbols of fellowship, or covenant, have always been pre-eminent in value. Yet even these instances tell only of covenant or fellowship between man and man, man and woman, nation and nation. What of fellowship or covenant with God Himself? These two symbols are like Everest among the mountains.

Yet there are other mountains. It seems to me a mistake to isolate the Sacraments. They are related to the whole Christian life. The word ' Sacrament ' may be properly used of many other rites. It may be rightly used of all nature, if the Christian finds it all to be the garment of God. Sometimes a great gulf is fixed between the two Sacraments and such other ordinances as the public worship of God, meetings for prayer, meetings for fellowship. This seems to me to be a mistake. Devotional life should be a whole, and it is wrong to pit one part of it against another. The Sacraments are not isolated in the life of the Christian, but part of it. Of course, this is so in fact in the life of all Christians who take religion seriously, but in discussion Sacerdotalists sometimes draw a very sharp line between the Sacraments and every other act of Christian worship. This seems to me to be both a theoretical and a practical mistake.

The two Sacraments have another distinction. It is a quality of many symbols of covenant that they *assert* a fellowship which is at other times *assumed*. It is said that at the older Universities it is usual to ' shake hands ' only twice a term—once at the beginning and once at the end. These twin acts assert a fellowship that is assumed for the rest of the term. It is the same when two acquaintances shake hands at the beginning and end of a conversation. Similarly, the signature of a treaty between nations asserts a covenant that thereafter is assumed. So, too, a wedding is the assertion of a fellowship that is assumed from that day forwards ' till death do part ' the two whom it binds. Yet it is not merely assumed, for every kiss is its re-assertion. The same is true of the two Sacraments. Baptism is the assertion of the beginning, and the Eucharist of the continuity, of a fellowship between Christ and Christian men that is at other times assumed.   It is assumed, for instance, in the other five rites sometimes called ' Sacraments.'   It is assumed in every act of Christian worship, in every prayer-meeting, in every fellowship meeting.   It is assumed by ardent Christians in the whole of life.   Symbols of assertion are peculiarly necessary, for men forget.   They need such symbols most of all when their fellowship is with an unseen Person. [1]

The Sacraments, then, are unique as ordinances of Christ Himself, as symbols of covenant with Him, as asserting a companionship that is at other times taken for granted.   It will be seen that much here builds upon the discussion in the second chapter.   There is no need at this point, perhaps, to do more than state that the two Sacraments, when faithfully received, nourish the fellowship that they express.   It will, I hope, be clear already, and clearer still below, that it is possible, and indeed easy, to be an Evangelical Christian and to think greatly of the Sacraments.   If one does not say that they are almost everything, he is not reduced to saying that they are almost nothing.

B. Baptism in the New Testament

It will be convenient to trace the New Testament references to the Sacrament of Baptism in a roughly chronological order, taking first the two or three places where the word occurs of ritual ' washings ' or purifications among the Jews, next the references to Baptism during our Lord's life, and last the references to the use of Baptism in the Apostolic Church.

Little need be said under the first head.   There is no

This is drawn out more fully on pp. 178 ff.

doubt that the literal meaning of the word ' baptism ' is
' dipping.' It was used of ritual purification, whether of
persons or things, by the Greek-speaking Jews. Our
Lord refers to ' baptisms of cups, and pots, and brazen
vessels '[1] as a Pharisaic practice, going on to declare that
' nothing from without a man . . . can defile him.'
This passage has some bearing, perhaps, upon our present
subject. It is difficult to believe that a teacher who
taught so emphatically the primacy of inward or spiritual
things would Himself institute a ritual practice that
should ensure or guarantee a spiritual boon. This,
however, is only to refer again in a particular instance to
the general attitude of the Bible, and of the Christ as the
consummator of Bible teaching, to ritual. In the same
context, and in the Epistle to the Hebrews, there are
references to the Jewish habit of ' baptizing ' the hands,
or the body generally, in certain acts of ritual.[2] It is
clear that here the use of the term is symbolic. There
is no hint that these ' baptisms ' were themselves supposed
to ' confer ' purity. Or, if some Pharisees behaved as if
they thought so, it is precisely this idea that our Lord
condemns.

It seems likely that in New Testament times Gentiles
who wished to become Jews were baptized, but the
forerunner of Jesus, John, was called ' the Baptist '
because he gave a new significance and prominence to the
rite. He baptized Jews, not Gentiles. Something else,
however, is more to the present purpose. When any one
was baptized by John, two things went together—an
outward sign and a spiritual experience. The outward
sign was immersion at the hands of the Prophet ; the
inward experience was repentance ' unto the remission of
sins.'[3] With the rite there went also ' confession of sins.'[4]
It is clear, I think, that John baptized adults only, or at

---

[1] Mark vii. 4. [2] Heb. ix. 10 ; cf. Luke xi. 38.
[3] Mark i. 4. The very phrase here marries the experience and the symbol.
Cf. Mark xvi. 16 ; Acts ii. 38. [4] Mark i. 5.

the least that normally he baptized adults. Few or none
would go to his baptism unless they were already conscious
of their sinfulness and their need for forgiveness. Jesus
Himself condemned ' the chief priests and elders of the
people ' because they did not ' repent ' and ' believe '
John.[1] Again, we read that ' the Pharisees and the
lawyers' were ' not baptized of [John].'[2] Men who thought
they had no need to repent would not accept his baptism.
In other words, we have here an instance where the rite
and the experience which it expressed are so closely blent
that they could be treated as one thing. We have also a
rite that would no doubt intensify and nourish the experience that it expressed. But no one suggests that the rite
was essential to the experience, or that merely to submit
to the rite would ensure or ' convey ' the experience. We
may reverently add the story of Jesus' own baptism.
For Him there was an accompanying spiritual experience,
though not an experience of repentance, for the sinless
had no need to repent. The ' voice from heaven ' gives
a clue about the nature of the experience. Our Lord
now entered consciously into the full knowledge of His
unique Sonship, and so of His unique mission. His
baptism expressed an experience that had been forming
for thirty years. He was Son of God from birth, but
He only fully knew it now. Again, only now did He know
fully what kind of life the Son of God must live for the
sake of sinners. It would be out of place here to expound
the passage further. Jesus' submission to baptism at
once expressed and intensified an experience and conviction. But did it work a work of ' grace ' in Him
ex opere operato ? It may here be noted that later Jesus
used the word ' baptize ' in a purely metaphorical way of
a still deeper experience—in the phrase, ' I have a baptism
to be baptized with, and how am I straitened till it
be accomplished.'[3] A rite, and the experience that it

Matt. xxi. 23–32.   [2] Luke vii. 30.   [3] Luke xii. 50.

signifies, may be so closely knit that the name of the rite, even when used in metaphor, may stand, as here, as the name of the experience.

We may turn next to the passages where the baptism of John and the baptism of Jesus are contrasted. The contrast appears first in the words of the Baptist, ' I baptized you with water ; but He [that cometh after me] shall baptize you with the Holy Ghost.'[1] Matthew and Luke add the words ' and with fire.'[2] According to the Acts of the Apostles, Jesus Himself contrasted the two baptisms in the same way.[3] Yet while there is here a contrast, there is also a connexion. It is implied that the baptism of John was an incomplete thing, and that Jesus was to complete it. But what was He to complete—the rite, or the experience that it expressed ? There is universal agreement that, for those who followed Jesus in His lifetime and who persisted in following Him even through the catastrophe of Calvary, the ' baptism with the Holy Spirit ' was at Pentecost. Indeed, the Book of the Acts says as much.[4] We are told that their number was ' about a hundred and twenty.'[5] It might be claimed that at Pentecost the Holy Ghost ' filled ' only the Twelve, though it seems more natural to apply the word to the whole group. But, whether it be the Twelve or the ' hundred and twenty,' was there any baptism with water for those who were filled with the Spirit at Pentecost ? We read, indeed, about those who ' were pricked in their hearts ' that Peter said unto them, ' Repent ye, and be baptized every one of you in the name of Jesus Christ unto the remission of your sins ; and ye shall receive the gift of the Holy Ghost,'[6] but what of the first group itself ? For some of them the baptism of John ' unto remission of sins ' seems to have sufficed ; others of them may not have been baptized by water at all. This means, of

[1] Mark i. 8.   [2] Matt. iii. 11 ; Luke iii. 16.   [3] Acts i. 5, xix. 11, 16.
    [4] Acts i. 5, 8.   [5] Acts i. 15.   [6] Acts ii. 38.

H

course, that none of them was ever literally 'baptized into the name of Jesus Christ.' Again, even if we take it that they had all received the baptism of John, this symbol and Pentecost were separated by an interval of months, or even years. In this instance, at least, the 'grace' was given apart from the rite. And, indeed, these first disciples did not submit to distinctively *Christian* Baptism at all.

We may now turn to the passages about Baptism in the Fourth Gospel. Not long ago it was usual to refer almost all its teaching to a later period than Jesus' lifetime, but there are signs of a rebound from this extreme position. So far as I can judge, it seems likely that the *incidents* in the Fourth Gospel are historical, and that, while the *teaching* is sometimes expressed in the writer's words rather than in Jesus' own, and is expounded by him at greater length than Jesus expounded it, yet there is genuine teaching of the Lord in this Gospel. We ought therefore, I think, to ask whether the Sacramental passages in this Gospel can be given a meaning appropriate to the occasion with which the writer associates them. One or two of them are discussed also at a later point, since it seems to me that, whether they be Jesus' own teaching or the writer's, they bear a Sacramental and not a Sacerdotal interpretation. So far as Baptism is concerned, we note first that John's baptism is referred to in a way strictly parallel to the way of the Synoptic Gospels. It is treated as at once in contrast with Jesus' 'baptism with the Holy Spirit' and as preparatory to it.[1] We gather also that some of the chief of Jesus' disciples had been baptized by John.[2] Further, we read that Jesus Himself began to baptize while John was still baptizing,[3] and that, at least sometimes, Jesus' disciples baptized in His stead.[4] I suppose that a Sacerdotalist would not

---

[1] John i. 8, 15, 23–34 ; iii. 22–30. [2] John i. 35–42.
[3] John iii. 22–4. [4] John iv. 1 f.

maintain that this baptism ' conveyed ' the grace of the
Holy Spirit, anticipating Pentecost.[1]   Would he, then,
say that such baptized persons needed a second baptism
' with water ' in order that they might ' receive the Holy
Spirit ' ?   Here, as in the Synoptists, the rite and the
gift of the Spirit do not fall together.   Yet surely this
baptism, too, expressed and nourished some inward
spiritual experience.   What experience was it ?   In
all probability it was the same experience of repentance ' unto remission of sins ' that John's baptism
expressed.[2]   It would be easy to show that there are
here good instances of the phenomena that, as traced in
the second chapter, always attend the healthy use of
symbols.

We come now to the story of Nicodemus.[3]   Is it possible
to find a meaning for it that is appropriate to the situation
with which the writer connects it—the opening of Jesus'
ministry ?   Nicodemus comes before us as a ' Pharisee, a
ruler of the Jews.'   The latter phrase seems to mean
that he was a member of the Sanhedrin.[4]   In the Synoptic
Gospels, as already noted, it was precisely such men that
Jesus upbraided with refusing the baptism of John.[5]
They tell us also that Jesus rebuked the hypocrisy of the
Pharisees.   But they also say and imply that He taught
that His disciples must surpass the ' righteousness ' of the
sincere Pharisee.   The very passage from which this
phrase is quoted[6] preludes the famous comparison in the
Sermon on the Mount where Jesus sets His ' I say unto
you ' over against, ' It was said to them of old time.'
Throughout the comparison He insists on one truth—
that there must be righteousness of motive as well
as righteousness of behaviour ;   that the outward is
insufficient without the inward.   In brief, He keeps on
saying what the Fourth Gospel epitomizes in a single

---

[1] Cf. John vii. 39.   [2] Cf. Mark i. 15.   [3] John iii.
[4] Cf. John vii. 50.   [5] Cf. John iv. 1.   [6] Matt. v. 20.

sentence, ' Ye must be born again.' The metaphor was extreme, yet was not too extreme, for in the Seventh and Eighth of Romans we watch the ineffective struggle of a sincere Pharisee to attain to this inward kind of righteousness and his immediate success when once he ' believed on ' Christ. So far Jesus' words to Nicodemus agree with His Synoptic teaching.

Again, we have seen that both the Baptist and Jesus said the same thing in yet another way by calling all men to two baptisms—the baptism of repentance and baptism with the Holy Spirit. They spoke of both of these before Pentecost. In the one baptism there was a literal dipping in water ; in the other and greater ' baptism ' there was no such literal rite. Luke and Matthew, indeed, draw attention to this very difference by adding ' with fire ' to their accounts of the Baptist's words. Why should not Jesus be saying the same thing to Nicodemus ? Why should He not say, ' Except you repent, and show your repentance by coming to baptism, and except you go farther and receive the Holy Spirit, you cannot enter into the Kingdom of God ' ? It is worth notice that at this one point the Fourth Gospel uses the Synoptic phrase, ' the Kingdom of God.' It seems to me that this interpretation suits the narrative of the other three Gospels, and that there is no need to suppose that the Fourth Gospel falls here into an anachronism, and describes Apostolic baptism before it occurred. It describes accurately what happened at the beginning of Jesus' ministry. But, if this exposition be correct, does it not follow that when Jesus said, ' Except a man be born of water and the Spirit,' He used the phrase ' born of water,' not for the mere rite, but for the experience of repentance and its appropriate rite considered as one ? In the baptisms of that day the two would always go together. No Jew would submit to a new rite—and to a rite that acknowledged the insufficiency of his old Law—for mere

' form.' It is a good instance of the true marriage of
symbol and experience. But does any one claim that the
baptism of John, or even the baptism of Jesus and His
disciples, itself ' conveyed ' repentance ? The gift of the
Spirit, at least in the view of the writer of the Fourth
Gospel, was not yet. [1] We have still the Sacramental, and
not the Sacerdotal, use of symbols.

We pass now to the references to Baptism after
Pentecost. There are two passages in the Gospels that
may be named here. One of them occurs at the
end of Matthew, [2] the other in the present ending of
Mark. [3] It is not unlikely that in phraseology both
of these bear the mark of anachronism, and that they
belong therefore to the group of Apostolic references
to Baptism that we have now reached. [4] When the
first is compared with passages in the Acts, it follows
that at some early period a change was made in the
formula of Baptism, or that more than one formula
was used, for we have the two formulae : ' Into the
name of Jesus Christ,' and ' Into the name of the Father
and of the Son and of the Holy Ghost.' The time of
rigidity of rite had not yet come. The phrase in
Mark knits the experience and its symbol just in the
way that we shall presently find common in the Acts
and Epistles.

When the references to Baptism in these books are
examined, it seems clear, in the first place, that the
normal use was still the baptism of adults. There are,
indeed, two or three texts that do not certainly exclude
the baptism of infants, [5] but there can be no doubt that
in New Testament times, as always where Christianity
is a new religion, the great majority of Baptisms were
adult, and it is this kind of Baptism that the passages
in question have in view. Again, it is noteworthy that,

---

[1] John vii. 39.   [2] xxviii. 19.   [3] xvi. 16.
[4] For Matt. xxviii. 19, see also pp. 215 f.   [5] Acts xvi. 15, 33 ; 1 Cor. i. 16.

apart from a small set of passages where there is mere mention of the fact that certain people have been baptized,[1] two things go together. They are the two things of which I have already spoken—the outward and the inward. Of outward things there are four—the act of baptism by water itself, the use of ' the Name ' of the Lord Jesus, the ' laying on of hands,' and ' speaking with tongues ' ; to these ' prophecy ' must be added, if it be distinguishable from the last. There is, as I think, only one inward thing named, and it may be defined, as before, as a spiritual experience, but it is described in quite a number of ways, or, rather, on quite a number of sides. We read of repentance, of faith, of the remission of sins, of the receiving of the Spirit, and of a new kind of life.[2] Finally, in one passage we read of being ' baptized into one body,'[3] and other passages compare Baptism to circumcision, and to the escape of Noah and his family from the Flood.[4] More must be said about some things in this brief statement.

It seems clear that Baptism was the universal symbol of faith in Christ, and consequently of entry into His Church. Again, this Sacrament is everywhere treated as important. Its inclusion in a list like this—' There is one body and one Spirit . . . one Lord, one faith, one baptism, one God and Father of all '[5]—is a good instance. A single passage has, indeed, often been quoted on the other side by Evangelical Christians— ' Christ sent me, not to baptize, but to preach the gospel '[6]— but it seems to me that the context requires, not that Paul thought Baptism unimportant, but that he thought it unimportant *by whom* the rite was carried out. He tells the quarrelling Corinthians that it did not matter who

[1] e.g. Acts ii. 41, viii. 36, 38.

[2] The following passages will illustrate these statements : Acts ii. 38, 41, viii. 12 f., 36, 38, ix. 17 f., x. 44–8, xvi. 14 f., 31–4, xviii. 8, xix. 3–5, xxii. 16 ; Rom. vi. 1–11 ; I Cor. i. 13–17, xii. 13 ; Gal. iii. 26 f.; Col. ii. 11 f.; Heb. vi. 2.

[3] I Cor. xii. 13.   [4] Col. ii. 11 f. ; I Pet. iii. 21.   [5] Eph. iv. 4.   [6] I Cor. i. 17.

had baptized them, for they had all alike been baptized into one Name.

Of the four outward things named, one, the ' laying on of hands,' has already been discussed, and it is only necessary to say that it only occasionally occurs as accompanying Baptism,[1] and then as something even more intimately connected with the receiving of the Holy Spirit.   If one were to argue as rigidly from the letter of these passages as some have argued from others, it would follow that the gift of the Spirit comes, not by Baptism at all, but by Confirmation.   We may leave this subject, however, to be debated between the different Sacerdotalist Churches.   Of the other three outward things, two are constant—the use of ' the Name '[2] and immersion in water.   It has already been seen that the formula used varied, but it was always such as brought the baptized person into relation to the gospel of Jesus Christ.   It is not easy to say whether the fourth outward thing—' speaking with tongues '—always accompanied Apostolic Baptism or not.   It is mentioned twice.[3]   In the first passage it is named as the outward token that Cornelius and his comrades had received the Spirit, and there seems to be a similar implication in the second. Was it the universal token of this ?   If so, this token has long lapsed, and there are hints that, already in New Testament times, other signs of the Spirit's working were preferred to *glossolalia*.   Paul writes, for instance, to the Galatians, ' The fruit of the Spirit is love, joy, peace, longsuffering, kindness, goodness, faithfulness, meekness, self-control.'[4]   These things, however, apart at least from ' joy,' could not show themselves ' on the instant.' Was there any instantaneous token ?   What was it that so strongly impressed Simon Magus when the Holy Ghost ' fell upon ' the believers at Samaria ?[5]   Apparently

---

[1] Acts viii. 17–19, xix. 6 ; and perhaps Acts ix. 17 ; Heb. vi. 2.
[2] Yet see p. 117.   [3] Acts x. 44–8 xix. 3–5.   [4] Gal. v. 22 f.   [5] Acts viii. 18.

it was the *glossolalia*. The story almost says in as many words that there was some outward token.[1] But, whatever be the answer to this question, it is clear that ' speaking with tongues ' sometimes accompanied Baptism in Apostolic times, and that here Apostolic precedent is now ignored.   I have stated above that for me the Lord Jesus Christ's own institution of the two Sacraments makes them obligatory indeed.   I add here that I do not take any Apostolic precedent, particularly when there is no clear Apostolic direction, as necessarily imposing obligation upon later Christians.   Of the outward accompaniments of Apostolic Baptism, one, *glossolalia*, is gone ; a second, immersion, has given way to aspersion ; why should a third, the ' laying on of hands,' be reckoned a *necessary* ' confirmation ' of this Sacrament ?   It is a venerable rite ; it may be a valuable one ; any Church may make it obligatory on its members ; but it is neither essential to Christian experience nor obligatory on all Christians.   Neither it, nor Baptism, nor any other outward thing, uniformly accompanies the gift of the Spirit in the New Testament.

Turning, however, to the inward experience which, under various terms, is so frequently connected with Baptism, the first phenomenon that strikes us is the closeness of the connexion in the majority of passages.   I have said above that in a healthy society the outward and the inward always go together ; that they are so intimately blent that they can be spoken of as a single thing ; and that the outward symbol nourishes or intensifies the experience that it expresses. All these things are true of that healthy society, the first Church. It is one of the marks of many a new and small society that no one joins it except from conviction.   For new societies, if they are missionary, are usually unpopular, and the lukewarm do not join an unpopular sect.   It is

[1] Acts viii. 16.

true that the unpopularity of Christianity passed away in some places more quickly than in others, and that where it passed, the Church was speedily plagued with the thing known as ' nominal membership,'[1] yet it is also true that, as a rule, in New Testament times a man would only join the Nazarene sect under the pressure of conscience and the impulse of a new found faith in Christ. Under such circumstances the Baptism, of course of an adult, is a very heart-searching experience. Perhaps I may illustrate from a memory of my own. Years ago I was present at a service in a little Marathi Church in Bombay. It stood like a light in the midst of a densely crowded part of that heathen city. I did not know the language, yet the spirit of worship was so intense that I could not but ' hear in my own tongue ' the word of the Spirit. Presently the Indian minister gave a sign, and a tall man rose in the middle of the church and stepped firmly down the aisle. He stood while the minister baptized him ' into the Name,' and gave him ' the right hand of fellowship.' He had been in long training for that day, and in heart he was already a Christian. He was now ' confessing ' his Lord by outward symbol. But there was no question of ' mere symbol.' The symbol intensified and developed the experience that it expressed. As he turned to find his way back to his seat, his feelings overcame him, up he threw a hand, and out there rang a Marathi ' Hallelujah.' Some may call this ' sensational,' yet it is not more so than Pentecost. The New Testament Church was a light shining in dark places ; it was ' everywhere spoken against ' ; none joined it unless he had already begun to ' believe'; and, when he submitted to the ordeal of public Baptism—for it is an ordeal—he received the Holy Ghost. Symbol and experience may be so thoroughly blent that one can only say, ' What God hath joined, let no man put asunder.'

[1] e.g. Rev. iii. 15 f.

Now, it seems to me not only possible, but natural, to explain all the passages that the Sacerdotalist most frequently quotes in support of his account of Baptism, after the manner just illustrated. It may be true—I think it is true—that, if two or three passages be taken alone and interpreted literally, they can be made grammatically to bear the Sacerdotalist construction. But, when a passage admits of more than one interpretation, surely that interpretation is to be preferred which suits best the nature of the book in which it occurs. In the last chapter I tried to show the general attitude of the Bible to the question of the relation of the inward and the outward, the spiritual and the symbolic, to each other. Is a literal interpretation of a very few passages to outweigh all this, when another interpretation is possible, and even natural? One of the favourite texts of the Sacerdotalist is the saying in the Fourth Gospel, ' Except a man be born of water and of the Spirit, he cannot enter into the Kingdom of God.'   I have already given my own account of this passage.   If, however, it be maintained that there is here anachronism, and that the reference is to the Christian custom of Baptism, as it was exercised after Pentecost, then it seems to me that there is here just an instance of the close association of symbol and experience that I have just tried to describe.   To a man in Ephesus, say, in the first century, Baptism and the receiving of the Spirit were indeed two indissoluble things, for no man would face the ordeal of Baptism unless he had already begun to enjoy the experience.   The two were as closely knit as laughter with merriment or tears with sorrow.   There is evidence of this in the repeated mention of ' faith ' as preparatory to Baptism or as accompanying it.[1]   Again, when Peter, having said of Noah that he was ' saved by water,' adds ' which also in the antitype doth now save you, even baptism,' he

---

[1] e.g. Acts viii. 12 f., xvi. 31-4, xviii. 8, xix. 3-5 ; Gal. iii. 26 f. ; Col. ii. 12.

does not seem to me to mean that Baptism is the literal cause of salvation. He is speaking after the same fashion as a minister of to-day would be speaking if he said to a married pair, ' Marriage has made you one,' or as a man who wishes to end an estrangement says, ' Give me your hand.' Just as there is no suggestion in the last two phrases that the wedding-ring or the hand-grip is the cause of love or of friendship, so there need be no suggestion in the first phrase that Baptism is the cause of salvation. This is the more so as the context goes on to prefer the inward to the outward, ' the appeal of a good conscience towards God ' to ' the putting away of the filth of the flesh.' It seems to me, again, that the passages in Paul that are most often quoted bear a similar sense. Perhaps two may stand for the rest.[1] In a Chapter already quoted we read, ' For in one Spirit were we all baptized into one body, whether Jews or Greeks, whether bond or free ; and were all made to drink of one Spirit.'[2] Here Paul assumes that the spiritual experience and its Sacramental expression went so uniformly together that they could be treated as one, and he applies this to enforce the practical truth with which he was immediately dealing—that, through the common experience of the Spirit, Christians are organically one, are a true society— are, indeed, *the* true society, the Christian Church. The other passage is the first paragraph of the Sixth of Romans. Here the Apostle draws a parallel between the rite of Baptism and the death and resurrection of our Lord. The sentence where he names Baptism runs as follows :

[1] In Acts xix. 1–7, Baptism ' into the name of the Lord Jesus ' is *added* to John's baptism. As already noted (pp. 113 f.), this was probably not so in earlier days. Perhaps there is here one of the tokens that, while Jesus deliberately carried on the movement that John had begun, and while their unity seemed obvious to their contemporaries (e.g. Mark vi. 16), yet at a later date their bands of disciples fell asunder, John's ' disciples ' claiming for him a pre-eminence over Jesus that he had not claimed for himself (cf. John i. 6 f., 15). This schism, however, may only have been incipient in the period covered by Acts (Acts xviii. 25), for it is not clear that Apollos was ever baptized into the name of Jesus (Acts xviii. 26).

[2] 1 Cor. xii. 13.

' Or are ye ignorant that all we who were baptized into Christ Jesus were baptized into His death ? We were buried, therefore, with Him through baptism into death ; that, like as Christ was raised from the dead through the glory of the Father, so we also might walk in newness of life.'[1] It lies on the surface that the passage is highly figurative. No one supposes that in Baptism the Christian dies a physical death, and literally rises again. In a vigorous metaphor Paul is saying what he says elsewhere in another : ' If any man is in Christ, there is a new creation.'[2] And he knows that, both when he himself was baptized, and when many and many a Roman Christian was baptized, the outward symbol coincided with the climax of an inward experience. He knows that the mere act of Baptism was a true and high ' means of grace,' as such acts always are when rightly used. But, in face of his lifelong agony against the Jewish doctrine of the sufficiency of that outward thing, Law, and in face of his comparison, in a parallel passage, of Baptism to a ' circumcision not made with hands,'[3] is it credible that Paul is here speaking literally ? To insist that he is, is to insist that he should stultify himself. Baptism may be an occasion of the gift of the Spirit without being its cause.

There remain, to support the exegesis here urged, the two well-known passages in the Book of the Acts where the spiritual experience and the Sacramental sign occur apart. In one passage[4] the rite comes first, in the other[5] the experience. In both the usual and healthy coincidence is lacking. It seems to follow that we rightly speak of their proper relation as of coincidence, and not as of cause and effect.[6]

---

[1] Rom. vi. 3 f.   [2] 2 Cor. v. 17.   [3] Col. ii. 11 f.
[4] Acts viii. 12, 17.   [5] Acts x. 45-8.
[6] The passage in the Epistle to the Hebrews where Baptism is mentioned (Heb. vi. 1 f.) is so allusive that it is susceptible of more than one interpretation. seems to me quite possible to expound it in accordance with the Sacramental

C. Infant Baptism

Children are the most delightful creatures in the world, yet, as soon as the subject of childhood enters any discussion, peculiar difficulties emerge. This is especially true in the realm of psychology. ' Child psychology ' is a subject that is tantilizingly obscure. It follows that any theology that seeks to do justice to psychology, as modern theology increasingly does, will find peculiar difficulties when it speaks of childhood. Augustine is often distinguished as the first Christian teacher who seriously sought to give any account of the psychology of the Christian life. His difficulties when he came to speak of unbaptized infants are well known. And every theology since his day has found itself faced with peculiarly intractable problems as soon as it has sought to give its account of the theology of childhood. Not the least intractable is the problem of the relation of symbols and Sacraments to children.

The chief ground of these difficulties is not hard to discern. The people who seek to explain phenomena, and to build theories on their explanations, are adult. They work with the adult mind. The psychologist in particular has only direct cognisance of his own adult experience.

principle. The writer says that he will ' leave the word of the beginning of Christ '—i.e. that he will go on from the things with which the Christians of his day began. He then gives specimens of these things under three heads— those ' foundation ' things, repentance and faith ; teaching (reading διδαχήν) of baptisms and laying on of hands ; of the resurrection of the dead and eternal judgement. It seems to me that ' baptisms and laying on of hands ' are to be taken together as the twofold symbol of admission into the Church. Where Christianity is a missionary religion, preparation for Baptism always plays a very great part in the life of the Church—and this whether the Church be of the Sacramental or the Sacerdotal type. Among the very first things, therefore, in which the Hebrew Christians would have been instructed there would fall the meaning of the twofold sign of admission to the Church. It will be noted that I think that ἀρχή means ' beginning ' literally, and not ' principle.' The plural, ' baptisms,' is difficult on any interpretation. If the disciples of John the Baptist and of Jesus were drawing apart among the Jews at this time (see footnote on p. 123), it may have been that Hebrew Christians were specially instructed in the difference between the baptisms of Jesus and John.

It is only by memories of his own past childhood and the observation of the ways of children about him that he can pry into the mind of childhood at all, and both methods easily mislead. For the psychological difference between a child and adult is that between a being that is gradually becoming a person and a being that has already become one. These differences, of course, are at their maximum when the comparison is drawn between an adult and a newly-born child. At later stages even a child seems to be fully conscious, and is already beginning to be free. In its very first days it is easy to assert that it is conscious, but very difficult to give any clear meaning to the assertion. It is easy, again, to say that it is already ' in a sense ' a free agent, but who can define the ' sense ' ? We say that the child is conscious, yet add confidently, ' It does not know.' We say that it has begun to be free, yet are sure that it does not know how to choose ! In the discussion above—to turn to the instance before us— we have spoken wholly of adult life. Not a little of the second chapter, for instance, does not apply to infancy at all. Or, at the least, it does not apply to a child a few days old, if the child be considered as what it is, not as what it is becoming. To say more about the general subject would take us too far from our immediate topic. The pertinent question emerges : What is to be said about Infant Baptism ?

If I understand the Sacerdotalist answer aright, it asserts that by the act of Baptism itself, if properly administered by a right person, ' grace ' is given to the child, and by this ' grace ' it becomes a child of God. It seems to me that this doctrine has no warrant either in the New Testament or in psychology. I cannot but think that it crept into the Church from the so-called Mystery Religions and other such heathen sources in the days when the Church was far too susceptible to their influence. If the word ' magical ' be used in the popular and not in the scientific sense, it seems to me difficult to refuse it to this concept. The doctrine has no analogies in the rest of human life. It may indeed be said that the use of such symbols as words, integrated in language, begins to influence a child long before we can trace their influence, but this is not a true parallel. No one suggests that the symbol called a word, if used only once a few days after a child is born, would seriously influence it at all. It is by the constant repetition of the symbols of a language through the plastic years of childhood that a great language influences the mind and character of every child that hears it spoken. Baptism, on the other hand, is not repeated. The only refuge for the theory, so far as I can see, is to postulate a ' miracle ' in every Baptism, and to postulate it, as I try to show below,[1] in an outworn and non-Christian sense. I state these opinions without further argument, because my purpose now is not primarily controversial.

For the Evangelical Christian a question arises that does not trouble the Sacerdotalist. It is : ' Ought Baptism to be reserved for adults, or may children be baptized? ' At first sight it may seem clear that the principles examined above require that only adults should be baptized, for the question at once emerges : ' If a symbol is used to express and nourish a given experience, why use it when the experience is not there ? ' One large Evangelical Church, the Baptist, baptizes none but adults. All the other Evangelical Churches practise Infant Baptism. For myself I have no doubt that the latter are right. At the same time, I do not think that the difference between other Evangelical Christians and the Baptists is as great as some suppose, for it seems to me that in Infant Baptism the symbol has not entirely the same significance as in Adult Baptism. It is necessary to say something on certain theological subjects before I

[1] See the Appendix.

can make my meaning clear, but I will make the statement as summary as possible. As already shown, it seems to me clear that, apart from a doubtful text or two, the New Testament always speaks of Adult Baptism. Yet it seems to me, too, that the Church was guided aright when it passed to the practice of baptizing the children of Christian homes, whether this was done in New Testament times or not.

It is necessary at this stage to recall that Christian symbols are the symbols of a fellowship in which three parties are involved. These three are God, the Church, the individual Christian. I must add summarily some theological truths about each of the three.

There is perhaps no theological doctrine so generally taken for granted by Christians to-day as that of the Universal Fatherhood of God. In other words, we readily assume that God is the Father, not only of every Christian, but of every man. There is not much direct evidence of this in the New Testament, yet there too it is taken for granted. What does this Fatherhood mean ? It means, no doubt, that God gives to all men food and shelter and clothing and all the good things of ' this life '—but does it mean no more ? The word 'fatherhood' implies fellowship, and in every true human home there is a fellowship of mind with mind and soul with soul that belongs to the psychical and not to the physical realm. Surely this is so with the Great Father too. But how does He seek this fellowship with His children ? Some New Testament texts suggest the answer ' Through the Son.' For instance, the writer of the Fourth Gospel says of the Logos, ' In Him was life, and the life was the light of men.'[1] In current Christian thought the answer is more readily, ' Through the Holy Spirit.' This is a part of the doctrine of Immanence. ' Every thought of holiness,' we sing, ' Is His alone.' Whether we think of the Son or

[1] John i. 4.

the Spirit or of both here, the truth remains that God does seek, and in some degree hold, fellowship with every man, for He is every man's Father.

When does this fellowship begin ? Well, when does an ' earthly father ' begin to hold fellowship with his child ? Here we strike on that elusive word ' influence.' No one can say what it is, yet we all know that in some unknown way one ' personality ' may ' get at ' and change another ' personality,' and we call this process ' influence.' In this sense every human father ' influences ' his child. At what moment does he first do so ? No one would suggest that his ' influence ' does not and cannot begin until the child is conscious of the ' influence ' and consents to the fellowship. Some would say that through heredity a father ' influences ' his child even before birth. Certainly he begins to ' influence ' it at birth through the environment of the home that he makes. This is obviously so in the physical realm, and here it is difficult, and even impossible, to differentiate between the physical and psychical. There is a fellowship between a father and a child from the child's birth. It is true that, at this stage, the child's part in the fellowship is chiefly receptive, yet it is there. One may add other questions about ' influence.' How soon does music begin to ' influence ' a child ? Surely as soon as it hears a single note. How soon do the things called ' race ' and ' nationality ' begin to ' influence ' a child ? The physical differences between an English and a Hottentot home begin to ' make a difference ' to a child from the moment of birth, and even before it ; are the differences wholly physical ? It seems clear that, though we know so little about ' influence ' and about child psychology, yet we do know that many things ' influence ' a child's mind and incipient ' personality ' from birth or earlier. Are we to say that race and nationality and music and human parentage ' influence ' a child at that stage, and that God cannot and does not ?

I

To ask the question is to answer it. The fellowship between God and man begins at birth.

Some of the old theologians rightly used the word ' grace ' of the Godward side of this fellowship, even at this its first stage, and, to distinguish it from ' grace ' of other kinds, called it ' prevenient grace.' It comes in some degree to every man, whether baptized or not. The use of the word ' grace,' however, suggests the word ' sin,' for ' grace ' is love at work for sinful man. Similarly the phrase ' prevenient grace ' suggests the phrase ' original sin.' This last has been supposed by some to be ' an exploded doctrine,' but like some other such doctrines it survives explosions. There is no need, however, either to define or discuss the phrase here. For myself I prefer ' racial degradation.' It is a fact that not only good things but evil ones come to every child because he is born into our present human society. For theological purposes it does not matter whether they come by heredity or environment or both. It suffices that willy-nilly they do come to every child born into the sin-stricken society called mankind. Some trace them to birth, and some to nurture, but all agree that there do come both good ' influences ' and evil ' influences ' to every child of man, merely because he is a child of man—or, to use another term, merely because he is inevitably societary. There is truth behind the old theological terms ' original sin ' and ' prevenient grace.'

Of course these two sets of societary ' influences,' the good and the bad, operate upon all men, not only at birth, but throughout life. This fact may help us toward the answer to the question : ' Which of the two is the stronger ? ' The argument of the First of Romans, for instance, requires that even among the *heathen* the ' influence ' of the Holy Spirit in the ' conscience ' is initially stronger than that of sin. Some may doubt this, however. It seems clearer that for the ancient *Hebrew* the good ' influence ' that came to him from the Israel into which he was born was greater than the evil one. Paul implies this in his own way when he says, ' They drank of a spiritual rock that followed them, and the rock was Christ.'[1] It will be seen that in this text he represents the Son as ' influencing ' men before the Incarnation. It is clearest of all, however, that, if a child be born in a *Christian* home, the good societary ' influences ' that come upon it willy-nilly are stronger than the evil ones. Sometimes theologians have written as though the things called ' prevenient grace ' and ' original sin ' were the same for every child. On the account just suggested, clearly this is not so. Whatever be the reason, God does not treat every child in the same way. By His strange providence one is born into a Christian environment, another into a Pariah environment. Whatever may be said of the second instance, in the first it seems clear that the good societary ' influences ' that affect the child are, on the balance, the greater. Initially, that is, ' grace ' is stronger than ' sin.' Whatever may be said of others, a child born into a Christian home begins life in the family of God. If ever it is found in the ' far country ' of the great Parable, it is not because it was born there, but because the child itself has chosen, at a later stage of life, to go away there. So far, therefore, as God's part in the fellowship that makes Christianity is concerned, it seems right that its symbol should come at birth rather than later.

It may be said, however, that symbols exist for the benefit of man and not of God, and it may have been noticed that already, by implication, we have passed to the second of the three parties to the Christian fellowship, the Church. For such phrases as ' the family of God ' have been used, and they define what the Church seeks to be, and indeed already begins to be. In the second

[1] 1 Cor. x. 4.

it is appropriate and advantageous that, when the time of choice comes, there should be a second rite to mark the willing completion of fellowship, whether it be called Confirmation or not.[1]

To return to the advocacy of Infant Baptism—there is weight in the old question, ' If a child die, does it not go to heaven, and, if it be Christ's, why not say so ? ' It is impossible to believe that a dying child ' goes to hell,' even though it be the mitigated hell of the limbo of Augustine and other Fathers.[2] Nor has the Christian heart been wrong in turning to the story of Jesus and the ' Mothers of Salem ' in support of Infant Baptism. In it there is no direct reference to Baptism, of course, but the story does mean that children belong to Jesus. Again, the symbol of the kiss has already more than once been used as an illustration. Do a father and a mother postpone its use till their little one is old enough to understand what it means and to return it ? They kiss him as soon as he is born, for the symbol expresses and feeds their own love for him. It is the token of the fellowship of home. Baptism, rightly used, expresses and intensifies the fellowship of home with Christ. If the central thing in Christianity be fellowship with Christ, and if confession be but one of its consequences—however important and necessary a consequence—it seems to follow that Baptism, the symbol of the beginning of fellowship, should fall when the fellowship begins—that is, in the first days of life.

The Baptist delays Baptism until all the three parties to the fellowship can freely undertake it. I have suggested that other Evangelicals use it when two of them do so. But what if only one do so, and that one be

[1] The ' Service for the Recognition of New Members ' sometimes serves this purpose in the Wesleyan Methodist Church.

[2] For those who deny that it ' goes to heaven,' however, there are at least two other options—the child might cease to be, or another opportunity of becoming either good or bad might be given it in the Beyond.

God? What if there be no home or Church to undertake the duties of the Christian society? Shall a child then be baptized, if someone or other brings it for Baptism? Two answers are given in the instance of adults. Some missionaries baptize all who seek Baptism, whether the Church is able to shepherd them or not. An increasing number, however, refuse to do so. Unless the Church is willing and able to undertake its part, they say that to baptize is only to manufacture ' nominal Christians.' So far as I can see, they are right. Dr. Arnold was not wrong when he declared that the wholesale Baptisms of the Northern peoples of Europe by the first missionaries in those lands has proved one of the capital disasters of Christendom. Unhappily the error has been repeated in later times, for instance in the Southern parts of America. Christian symbols denote a relation to other Christians as well as to God. Where there is no church, therefore, there should be no Baptism. The answer thus given for the adult, seems to apply also to the child.

Finally, what is the exact difference made in the account of symbol when the term is used of Infant Baptism? On the account given above, the normal use of symbols is both societary and individual, for normally the two are complementary. When symbols are used in relation to infants, however, the societary element is paramount, and, on one account of child psychology, even sole. A wholly societary symbol, however, may yet be a very valuable one.[1]

---

[1] I have not discussed the change from immersion to aspersion as the method of Baptism. To make such a change seems to me well within the competence of the Church.

V

THE SACRAMENT OF THE LORD'S SUPPER

A. The Question at Issue

All Christians grieve because they contradict one another about the Sacrament of the Lord's Supper. Just where they ought wholly to be one, there they struggle most! We dispute on ' holy ground ' ! Yet men do not strive about things for which they do not care ; they agonize for the things that are dear. In the early centuries of our era Christians strove together generation by generation about the doctrine of the Person of Christ. Some part of the story, at least, seems to us lamentable. Yet they did think the doctrine worth fighting about, and the best of them thought so because they loved the God-Man ' with all their heart and mind and soul and strength.' To-day the Lord's Supper is the centre of controversy just because both Sacramentalist and Sacerdotalist care so much about it. On both sides, when they have ' kept the feast,' they have met their Lord Himself. Each side sincerely believes that the other is committing a grievous error about it. They are sure to dispute. Yet they may try to dispute as Christians ought. I should like in this first paragraph to express my regret if, in anything I say below, I have misinterpreted or misunderstood the teaching of those with whom I disagree. And, while I see no way at present to reconcile our differences, I pray that our Lord will so enlighten us that we may none of us seek merely to prevail, but all endeavour continually to discover His way of reconciliation.

Perhaps my first task here is to define as clearly as I can the different doctrines of the Lord's Supper, or at least the types of doctrine that belong respectively to what I am calling the Sacramental and Sacerdotal schools. The centre of controversy, of course, is the phrases of our Lord, ' This is My body,' ' This is My blood.' Other New Testament texts are involved as well, but these two are not only central but typical. First, both schools say that they believe in the ' real presence.' Both, that is, say that in the Sacrament of the Lord's Supper our Lord Himself is ' really,' or ' objectively,' or ' actually ' present. Something more will be said below about the meaning of the first two of these adverbs. But it needs to be made clear that the Sacramentalist rejects the merely ' commemorative view ' of the Lord's Supper, so mistakenly ascribed to Zwingli. The Sacramentalist asserts that our Lord Himself is present in the Eucharist, that in the Lord's Supper there is a ' Holy Communion,' a true fellowship between Jesus Christ and His disciples. He is not an absentee. Further, the Sacerdotalist agrees with the Sacramentalist that Jesus is ' spiritually ' present. He would agree, too, I think, that, inasmuch as the spiritual is greater than the physical, our Lord's spiritual presence is of greater moment than His physical presence, in whatever sense the word ' physical ' is used. Indeed, only a Materialist could deny this. The Sacerdotalist adds, however, that it is not enough to say that Christ is spiritually present. He claims that our Lord is present also in a physical or material way. He says that in Christ's phrase, ' This is My body,' the last word must be taken literally. He holds that otherwise our Lord's presence in the Sacrament would be incomplete —that without His physical or bodily presence there is no guarantee of His spiritual presence at all. So we

reach the old contention that something belonging to
the outward or material or physical realm is needed in
order to guarantee the presence of something that belongs
to the inward or immaterial or spiritual realm.[1]

It is perhaps necessary here to point out that the words
' spiritual ' and ' subjective ' are not synonyms. Sometimes the opinion here called Sacramental is named
' merely subjective.' Is it too much to ask those who
use the last phrase to state clearly in which of its
several senses they use the term ' subjective '? An
up-to-date psychologist would, I suppose, say that the
' merely subjective ' is as non-existent as the ' merely
concave.' Just as ' concave ' and ' convex ' go together,
so do ' subjective ' and ' objective.' In both instances
the one implies the other. It is, however, possible that
a man should make a mistake about the objective counterpart of his subjective experience. He may think, for
instance, that a distant animal is a horse when it is really
a mule. In more extreme cases, he is said to be subject
to illusions, as when he mistakes his wife for the queen.
Now, the only true meaning of the phrase ' merely subjective,' when used about the Sacramental or Evangelical
account of the Lord's Supper, is ' illusory.'[2] ' Our friends
the enemy ' may not wish to use a word that seems rude,
but it is well to avoid the mists of ambiguities even at
this risk. What they mean by the phrase ' merely subjective,' so far as I can see, is that we think that the Christ
is present when we ' keep the feast,' but that He is not
present, or at least that our consciousness of His presence
is not sufficient guarantee of its own truth.

At this point the wide philosophic question emerges :
' What is the guarantee of truth ? ' All who follow Kant

---

[1] I have tried to state here the general opinion of Sacerdotalists,
but it is probably impossible to reduce the opinions of them all (or of
all Sacramentalists) to one agreed statement.

[2] When an experience is illusory, it is usually also merely individual, but
not always. Some writers seem to assume that ' subjective ' and ' individual '
are synonyms, but this is not so.

declare that to men the only possible guarantee of the truth of anything is that one or more men either think or practise it. This may be good guarantee, or bad guarantee, or sometimes good and sometimes bad, but in any case it is the only possible guarantee. It is not sufficient testimony, therefore, of the falsity of the Evangelical claim that Christ is really present when they gather at His table, to point out that its only proof is their own experience. But, to narrow the issue again, all Christians admit that the spiritual is sometimes the objective. Or, to put the same thing negatively, they admit that the objective and the material or physical are not synonyms. God Himself is not material, but ' pure Spirit '—yet surely He is objective. When Paul speaks of ' Christ in you, the hope of glory,' or writes, ' Nevertheless I live, yet not I, but Christ liveth in me,' is he not describing Someone who is objective, though purely spiritual ? As suggested above, here the Evangelical would identify the Son and the Spirit. Similarly, would not Sacerdotalists themselves assert that the Holy Spirit—when given, for instance, in Baptism or Ordination—is not ' merely subjective,' but objective and real, though by no means physical or material ? It is true that here the Sacerdotalist believes that something objective called ' grace ' is also given—something, as seen above, that is not merely a quality of a present Person—yet he denies that this ' grace ' is physical. It is certain that every one, except the materialist and a given kind of pantheist, believes that there are two kinds of objective beings, the one spiritual and the other material. The materialist denies the reality of the first, most pantheists deny the reality of the second ; but Christian thinkers assert the reality, and the objectivity, of both. To say, therefore, that the presence of Christ in the Eucharist is altogether spiritual, is not to deny its reality or objectivity ; this belief is not accurately described as ' merely subjective.'

For the Sacramentalist the Lord's Supper is the climax of symbolism, both psychologically and historically. When he partakes with his fellow Christians of the bread and wine, he believes that Christ is present—really and objectively, though only spiritually. He believes, further, that he has fellowship with his Risen Lord in the Sacrament. He finds that the symbols not only express this experience, but nourish it indeed. He finds, too, that at the Lord's Table there is a true ' Communion of Saints '—that in and through Christ he is one with all Christians, past, present, and future. Finally, he holds that to keep the Supper, as to observe Baptism, is obligatory as nothing of merely human authority can be, for he is bidden to the Lord's Table by the Lord Himself.

B. A SYMBOLIC ENVIRONMENT

Before examining the particular New Testament passages that name the Eucharist, I should like to draw attention to three pertinent facts of a general kind. The first is the least important. It might have been named in the second chapter, but it has peculiar relevance to the discussion of the Sacrament of the Lord's Supper. It is this,—There may be, there often is, a difference between the symbolic and the pictorial.[1] It is easy to illustrate from that great book of symbols, the Apocalypse. In its first Chapter there is a description of a great Being whom the seer says that he ' saw,' a Being having flaming eyes, brazen feet, and a sword thrusting out of His mouth ! All attempts to paint this figure fail. And they fail because the Being is not meant to be pictured. Every detail is symbolic : taken as symbolic, every detail is

[1] The history of the alphabet gives an illustration, if it be true that its letters were originally pictures.

significant ; all the details, taken together as symbolic, give the impression of wondering awe. Pictured, they are only grotesque. Similarly, when this writer says of the Holy City, ' The length and the breadth and the height thereof are equal,'[1] it is almost impossible to *picture* the City. One can imagine a city ' twelve thousand furlongs ' long, and ' twelve thousand furlongs ' broad, but what of a city ' twelve thousand furlongs ' high ? As a picture the description is bizarre, but as symbol it is triumphant. For the cube is an old symbol of perfection ; it was so used in the Holy of Holies of the ancient Temple of Israel ; this writer wants to say that in the New Jerusalem, not a secluded little shrine, but the whole city, thronging with men, is a Holy of Holies, and he says it by using the old and effective symbol. Symbols no doubt begin by being pictures ; often they continue to be so ; but, especially when a passionate writer betakes himself to symbol, the pictorial may be lost and only the symbolic remain—the symbolic and with it its indissoluble meaning.

The second fact is that Christian symbolism has centred in the Cross. It is well known that the Church has never been able to elaborate an entirely adequate doctrine of the Atonement. When all the thinkers of all the ages have said all that they can, we are still left with something experienced but inexplicable. In this dilemma the Christian, when his heart has been on fire with the great experience of redemption ' by the blood of the Lamb,' has sometimes tried to say in symbol what none can say in logic. In so doing he has often gone to lengths with symbolism that to the cold-blooded unbeliever, or even the cold-blooded believer, have seemed extravagant. It is easy to illustrate from the book already quoted. ' These are they which come out of the great tribulation, and they washed their robes, and made them white in the blood

[1] Rev. xxi. 16.

of the Lamb.'[1] Here there is another symbol that cannot be painted. In a picture such a 'washing' of robes would be repulsive. As symbolic, the words would not occur to any lukewarm Christian, and an unbeliever can readily wax cynical about them. But molten metal is not like cold slag! Here is a Christian whose heart is on fire with the experience of salvation. He knows that, in a way that he cannot explain, he has been cleansed from sinfulness because he has thrown himself upon a crucified Christ. And he uses a very expressive symbol of that high experience. There are similar uses of symbol in the devotional literature of many ages. It will suffice, perhaps, to add an instance or two from the hymns of to-day. Faber writes :

> Come, let us stand beneath the Cross :
> So may the Blood from out His side
> Fall gently on us drop by drop;
> Jesus, Our Lord, is crucified.

Or Cowper :

> There is a fountain filled with blood,
> Drawn from Immanuel's veins.

Or Toplady, uniting a fragment of Paul's symbolism with a fragment of John's :

> Rock of Ages, cleft for me,
> Let me hide myself in Thee ;
> Let the water and the blood,
> From Thy riven side which flowed,
> Be of sin the double cure,
> Cleanse me from its guilt and power.[2]

[1] Rev. vii. 14.

[2] *Hymns, Ancient and Modern*, Nos. 114, 633, 184. There is an extraordinary example in Vachel Lindsay's poem 'General William Booth enters into Heaven,' with its urgent refrain, ' Are you washed in the blood of the Lamb ? ' (quoted in *The Expository Times*, February 1927). It should be noted that many of these hymns were written by Evangelical Christians.

Here, again, the symbolic is not to be confused with the
pictorial ; here, again, to the onlooker, symbolism may
seem extravagant ; but here, again, it is the passionate
expression of a passionate experience. This is not
symbolism gone mad, but symbolism at its climax.
Whether in any of these instances its utmost verge has
been overstepped, I do not now inquire. It is sufficient
if I have shown that the Christian heart, when it struggles
to tell what it has found in the Cross, flings itself upon
the symbolic.

The last instances of the use of symbols have been from
Western writers, and it may seem that they could hardly
be surpassed, yet it is commonly agreed that the Eastern
mind more frequently and naturally turns to symbol
than the Western. There is perhaps no need to illustrate
this general statement. It is not always remembered,
however, that Jesus lived in the midst of an age that,
even in the East, was pre-eminently an Age of Symbol.
This is the third general fact that I wish to name. There
are two chief proofs of this. On the one side there is
Philo, and on the other the Apocalyptic literature. [1]
The former of these was the master of those Jews of
education who were seeking to make terms with Greek
thought. He found a way by interpreting the Old
Testament allegorically. In other words, he treated it
as a great arsenal of symbols. Paul, for instance, was
using Philo's method in a Christian fashion when he
wrote, ' They drank of a spiritual rock that followed them,
and the rock was Christ.' [2] On the other hand, among
the distinctively patriotic Jews, who had no wish to make
terms either with Greek culture or Roman imperialism,
the popular kind of writing was the Apocalypse. Its
vogue began with the Book of Daniel, written about a
century and a half before Christ. In our Lord's own day

[1] In the Book of Jonah there is probably a third type—Jonah symbolizing
Israel, the ' great fish ' the Captivity, and so on.
[2] 1 Cor. x. 4.

it was *the* popular kind of literature. Its era lasted until the second Christian century was far spent. To us many of its books seem uncouth. To many and many an enthusiastic Jew they were meat and drink. We have a specimen of them in the last book of our Bible. They teemed with symbolism. Beside the Christian Apocalypse, there are other New Testament passages of an Apocalyptic character. In them, too, the symbolic throngs. Indeed, ' Apocalyptic ' and ' symbolic ' are almost synonyms.

Neither our Lord Himself, nor the Apostles, nor the early Christians generally, attempted to escape from the atmosphere of symbolism in which they lived. This does not mean, of course, that they used symbols exactly as their contemporaries did. It is just as wrong to present them as passively following fashion, as it is to assume that they forsook it. As already seen, there are Christian writings that are Apocalyptic. In them the form does not differ much from that used by contemporaries, though, of course, the teaching that underlies the form differs greatly. There are other Christian writings, such as the Shepherd of Hermas, in which the type of symbolism has more tokens of originality about it. Paul goes his own masterful way in this style of writing, using the Philonic way now and then, or breaking out into Apocalyptic phrase, or leaving both alone, as his need demands. It is agreed that the writer of the Fourth Gospel is a great symbolist, though students differ about the extent of his symbolism. Some would reduce all the stories of miracle or ' sign ' in his book to mere allegory. I cannot follow them, but none the less this writer has a keen eye for a symbolic meaning,[1] and for him a miracle is not only a sign of power but a symbol of truth.[2] Our Lord Himself had His own way with symbol. He has, indeed, Apocalyptic passages, but these are not the most

---

[1] e.g. John ix. 7.   [2] e.g. John vi.

significant. In addition, He has two other uses of symbol, which yet are hardly two, but merge the one into the other. First, in His use of parable He is a great and original symbolist. But also, He had a matchless way of thrusting a parable into a sentence. Some write as if such phrases as ' I am the light of the world ' were peculiar to the Fourth Gospel. Yet it is not so. Maxims like ' Ye are the light of the world,' ' Whosoever smiteth thee on one cheek, turn to him the other also,' ' If thy right hand causeth thee to stumble, cut it off,' are common in the Synoptic tradition. Jesus was a master of symbolism, the greatest master in an age of masters.

Another point ought perhaps to be mentioned, though I have nothing to add to what others have said about it. On the Sacramentalist interpretation the phrases ' This *is* My body ' and ' This *is* My blood ' mean ' This is the symbol of My body ' and ' This stands for My blood.' Are there any parallels to such a use of the verb ' to be ' ? It seems to me that there are. There are two or three, for instance, in Ignatius, quoted later.[1] Within the Bible itself there are parallels in both Testaments. For example, when Joseph was interpreting Pharaoh's dreams, he said, ' The seven good kine *are* seven years ; and the seven good ears *are* seven years '[2]; similarly Ezekiel, in interpreting a vision, says, ' These bones *are* the whole house of Israel '[3]; and the seer of the Apocalypse speaks of ' Golden bowls full of incense, which *are* the prayers of the saints.'[4] Paul, again, writes, ' These women *are* two covenants,'[5] and our Lord Himself, in interpreting a parable says, ' The field *is* the world.'[6] Finally, in one of the accounts of the institution of the Eucharist itself we read, ' This cup *is* the new covenant in My blood.'[7]

[1] See pp. 166 f.   [2] Gen. xli. 26.   [3] Ezek. xxxvii. 11.   [4] Rev. v. 8.
[5] Gal. iv. 24.   [6] Matt. xiii. 38.   [7] 1 Cor. xi. 25.

K

C. THE INSTITUTION

There is some advantage in considering the Synoptic accounts of the institution of the Lord's Supper by themselves,[1] and then passing to the passages in other New Testament writings that refer to it. If both sets of passages are true to their historical environment, there is sure to be some difference between them, for the experience of the Eleven at the first Table would be neither exhaustive nor altogether typical. The right place to begin the investigation of the New Testament evidence is to seek an answer to the question, ' What did our Lord intend to teach His disciples as they sat round the table ? '

It seems to me likely that the meal was not a Passover —that the Fourth Gospel is right in putting it on the night before the regular keeping of that feast.[2] No doubt, when groups of people from a distance arranged with some dweller in Jerusalem for a room where they might ' eat the Passover,' this phrase meant that the room was at their disposal, not only for the one meal itself, but for the whole of the time usually spent at Jerusalem for the feast.[3] At their other common meals, the chief distinctive item would be the ' unleavened bread.' It is this that Jesus used as symbol of His body. If the meal were a real Passover, there would be a lamb on the table, but if so, He ignored it. Again, in using the wine as symbol of His blood, He used something that is not named in the Pentateuch at all. The use of the ' cup ' had been added in more recent times to the ritual. We reach, therefore, one of two conclusions—either the meal in Jewish eyes was not sacrificial at all, or, if it were, Jesus drew attention away from the distinctively sacrificial thing, the lamb, to something else. Further, when He

---

[1] The differences between the three Synoptists are not important for the present purpose.
[2] Cf. Luke xxii. 15.   [3] Matt xxvi. 17 ff.

' took a cup . . . saying, Drink ye all of it ; for this is My blood,'[1] He was deliberately departing from the sacrificial ritual, for to drink blood was an abomination to the Jew. Amid all the details of his elaborate ritual this use of blood never occurs.

Again, in the Upper Room, as at other moments of high tension, Jesus, the great Master of Symbolism, used both symbolic action and symbolic speech. In the incident of the feet-washing He used the first. A paragraph in Luke[2] exhibits the second. Let any one count the number of times that Jesus uses symbol in these few verses and he will see that Jesus' conversation at that moment thronged with symbolism. At last, indeed, He used it past their understanding. ' But now,' He said, ' he that hath no sword, let him sell his cloke, and buy one ' (R.V. marg.). They took Him literally. ' Lord, behold,' they said, ' here are two swords.' The atmosphere was alive with symbols. It seems to me that there were two others—' This is My body '; ' This is My blood.' Here those who were sitting with Him could not make a mistake ; they could not take Him literally.

But of what were the bread and wine symbolic ? I have said above that, even if the meal were sacrificial, Jesus drew attention away from its chief sacrificial feature to something else. What was this something else ? One of the most ancient and widespread symbols in the world is the common meal. It is the universal symbol of fellowship. It seems to me that Jesus' primary reference is to this, though there is a secondary reference to sacrifice, as will presently appear. To understand the reference to the symbol of the common meal it is necessary to try to think oneself back, say, into Peter's mind at the moment.

There can hardly be any doubt what was the dominant thought in the hearts of the Eleven. It was this :

---

[1] Matt. xxvi. 27   [2] Luke xxii. 24-38.

' This is the last time. After to-night all will be over, both with Him and His Kingdom. As for us, we may fall too, but, even if we escape, we can only be scattered and beaten men. We trusted that it had been He that should redeem Israel, but it's all over.' Before any separation of friends a last meal is often used as a tender symbol of something too deep for words ; but what of this last meal ?

Why do I call it ' last ' ? Because it seems to me that the common meal had meant a great deal in the fellowship of Jesus and His disciples. As we watch them wandering together through Palestine, we can see a pair of disciples now and again slipping away with the common ' bag ' to buy the bare food that they must have, and then we can see the whole group gather, under some tree or wayside shelter or in some friend's ' upper room,' to share the meal. The Lord is in the midst. He is Master of the feast. He has His own significant way of taking the bread and blessing and breaking—so significant that, after His Resurrection, two disciples could recognize Him by this gesture. These common meals have been the daily symbol of a fellowship that has deepened and deepened until now it is dearer than life. They have been the focus of each day's communion with Jesus. And after to-night there will never be another ! The Fourth Evangelist tells us that because Jesus said, 'I go away,' sorrow ' filled [their] heart.'

What help had our Lord to give to men in this despair ? If we may take the teaching of the discourse that the Fourth Evangelist places at this point as any guide at all—and I think that, however much of it is the exposition of the writer, he knew the situation that he set out to expound—Jesus had two things to say. The one of them may be put in these words : ' I am going away ' ; and the other in these : ' I am not going away.' This greatest Johannine passage[1] is an exposition of the second saying,

[1] John xiii.–xvii.

and of the truths implied in it, yet the first saying is
its necessary presupposition. In the Synoptic narrative,
as it seems to me, Jesus says the same two things, and
He says them both under symbols. According to Luke,
Jesus gave the disciples a first cup with this very message :
' I am going away for a while.'[1] According to the other
two Synoptists, He said this a little later.[2] The phrase of
all three is, ' I will no more drink of the fruit of the vine
until that day when I drink it new in the Kingdom of
God.' In other words—and whatever be the exposition
of this Apocalyptic phrase—Jesus told the disciples that
He would not be with them, as we say, ' in the body,'
for a while. He would not be physically present. But
He contradicted their deduction. They were thinking,
' Yes, and so the old, dear fellowship with Thee is over.
After to-night we shall have lost Thee, Lord.' ' No,' He
replies, ' I shall still be with you.' John tells us in what
way this is to be so. Jesus, he says, was to return in
' another Paraclete,' the Holy Spirit, who will be at once
the same Jesus and not the same. And John goes on to
say that this Paraclete will be the bond of the fellowship
that had begun to be theirs with Christ. The old fellowship is not to perish, but to continue and to mature.
' It is an advantage ' for them that Jesus should ' go
away,' for the Paraclete will perfect that fellowship
between Him and them and God that had begun
in Galilee and Judaea. The great Johannine passage rises to that ' high-priestly prayer ' that expounds
the mystery of this fellowship. Here there is no
symbol, but, as I think, its interpretation. Where
is the symbol ? In the Synoptists. ' This is My body ;
this is My blood '—it seems to me that Jesus is using
the symbol of the common meal to symbolize fellowship,
as all men have done. He tells the Eleven that their fellowship with Him is not to finish ' to-night.' Rather, it is to

---

[1] Luke xxii. 15–18.　　[2] Mark xiv. 25 ; Matt. xxvi. 29.

continue. They will discover that after His death they are not a scattered and defeated band, but that they begin then to be a victorious one. They will be strong at last ! And their fellowship with each other will continue and wax strong for the old reason—He will be there. He will be there just as really as if He were sitting there, flesh and blood, for them to see and handle. Indeed, He will be more really there. The continuance of their fellowship will betoken this, for without Him it would lapse. The common meal will continue, expressing the truth of His real presence and nourishing their actual fellowship with a present Christ. It has so continued and so nourished such a fellowship for nineteen hundred years. And, as tokens of this fellowship, as symbols of His presence, He takes the old symbols of their daily fellowship—the bread and wine of the common meal. ' Where they are,' He says, ' I am.' In brief, He was saying in symbolic form at the Last Supper what He elsewhere said without symbol : ' Wheresoever two or three are gathered together in My name, there am I in the midst of them.' An Eastern says : ' This is My body ; this is My blood ' ; a Western would mean the same if he said : ' He is here just as really as if He were here, body and blood.' The continuance of Christian fellowship demands as its ground the presence of the living Christ. On the other hand, the presence of the living Christ perpetuates the fellowship.

So far I have been considering the Lord's Supper chiefly from the point of view of a disciple who was sitting at the table with Jesus. But it had a meaning for the future as well as for the present, and our Lord was thinking of that meaning too. He was not only seeking to rescue His faithful few from immediate despair, but thinking of the future of His whole flock. To understand this part of His meaning it is necessary to examine His references to the sacrificial ritual of the Jews. It is, I think, clear that these references do not all suit any one part of the old ritual. It is natural, at first sight, to assume that His references are all to the Passover, as this was to be celebrated the next day, or was being celebrated at the very time of the Supper. But one of His phrases, ' unto remission of sins,' cannot be referred to it, as the Passover was not, and never had been, a ' sin-offering ' or ' guilt-offering.' For this phrase, taken by itself, we naturally turn to the ritual of the Day of Atonement. But, on the other hand, when Jesus said, ' Take, eat, this is My body,' His reference cannot be to the ritual of that day, for one of the marks of its ritual— and a very effective mark, if the whole scene of the day be realized—was precisely that in it none of the flesh of the victims was eaten. It was burnt ' without the camp,' as something so defiled by the sin that it symbolized that it could not be tolerated in the Holy Place at all. It is true that in some of the occasional sin-offerings and guilt-offerings the priests ate a part of the sacrifices, but even here the sinful, whose sin was thus expiated, did not share the meal. The eating of the flesh by the worshippers belonged to the so-called ' peace-offering,' and symbolized, as did the eating of the Passover lamb or kid, that the worshippers were in ' covenant ' with Jehovah, not alienated from Him by sin. Jesus, therefore, was not expounding any one piece of ritual, but using such illustrations from different parts of the ritual as suited His purpose.

What was that purpose ? We shall perhaps be able to answer the question if we notice that He referred to two Prophetic passages. For, so far as we can judge, it was not chiefly the ritualistic parts of the Old Testament on which His mind had fed at Nazareth for thirty years.[1] Rather, it was upon the Prophets and Psalms. Even

---

[1] It is calculated that of our Lord's quotations from the Old Testament, or allusions to it, fifty per cent. come from the Prophets and Daniel, twenty per cent. from the Psalms, and twenty-five per cent. from the Pentateuch (*Expository Times*, Vol. xxxviii., p. 337).

when He quotes the Law, He usually quotes the non-ritualistic parts of it, as in the story of His Temptation or in His saying about the ' two great Commandments.' What, then, are the two Prophetic passages of which He was thinking at the Last Supper? The first was Jeremiah's great oracle of the New Covenant. It is true that His phrase is, ' This is My blood of the covenant ' (or, with some manuscripts, ' the new covenant '), and that this seems to imply a reference to the story of the Twenty-Fourth of Exodus. But the reference to Jeremiah is surely there too. Jesus' new ' covenant ' is to supersede the ancient ' covenant ' of Exodus precisely because it fulfils the deep prophecy of Jeremiah. That prophecy had expressly asserted the failure of the Old Covenant, and demanded a new one of a spiritual, not of a ritualistic, kind. It puts ritual into a secondary place. It declares that there is need of an inward change, a spiritual re-creation, before the Israelite can enter into true fellowship with God. St. Paul and St. John tell us that it was to work this inward and spiritual change that our Lord died. He Himself knew this. He claims to inaugurate by His death the New Covenant that Jeremiah had foretold. He had not pondered His Bible in vain.

The other Prophetic passage to which He referred at the Supper was the Fifty-Third of Isaiah. He said, ' This which is written must be fulfilled in Me, And He was reckoned with the transgressors.'[1] I am one of those who think that this passage, more than any other in the Old Testament, influenced our Lord's whole life. It is only possible very summarily to give the evidence here. At His Baptism, as so many now hold, two Old Testament quotations were blent in ' the voice from heaven.' One of them referred to the Messiah : ' This is My beloved Son ' ; the other referred to the Suffering Servant of Jehovah, ' In whom I am well pleased.'[2] Of

---

[1] Luke xxii. 37.　　[2] Ps. ii. 7 ; Isa. xlii. 1.

course, I know that many to-day assert that Jesus did not understand that He must needs die until the days of retirement at Caesarea Philippi. I cannot think that He was so short-sighted. He had discovered something of His relation to God when a boy of twelve.[1] Eighteen years of brooding followed before He undertook His public task. Whatever the interpretation of the ' voice from heaven,' it seems to me all but certain that at that moment at latest He knew that He was to be a Messiah that died for others' sins. The words, ' Thus it becometh us to fulfil all righteousness,'[2] seem to be a second reference to the ' Righteous Servant.' Jesus must identify Himself with other men, even in their sinfulness, Himself remaining sinless, or He could not save them. He had learnt this from the Fifty-Third of Isaiah. He could not talk of this sad discovery, even to the Twelve, until they were ready to ' receive it.' He began to tell them the secret as soon as they were sure that He was the Messiah, and straightway Peter turned upon Him and ' rebuked Him.'[3] He made another reference to the great passage when He said, ' The Son of Man came not to be ministered unto, but to minister, and to give His life a ransom for many.'[4] It was under the impulse of such references that the first Christians came so soon and so naturally to call Him God's ' Holy Servant.'[5] And at the Supper the passage lay upon His soul. What was its message ? The Fourth Gospel tells us, ' Behold the Lamb of God, which taketh away the sin of the world.'[6] In other words, by dying for men Jesus expected to rid them of sin and to restore them to that fellowship with God for which they were created.

---

[1] Luke ii. 49. [2] Matt. iii. 15. [3] Matt. xvi. 16 ff.
[4] Matt. xx. 28. [5] e.g. Acts iv. 27, viii. 32 ff.
[6] John i. 29. If Jesus were thinking of the Fifty-Third of Isaiah at His Baptism, and if He had any considerable fellowship with John, it is not impossible that the saying is historical. On any interpretation, it is a further reference to the great prophecy.

We may now return to our Lord's references to the sacrificial ritual, for the Fifty-Third Chapter of Isaiah also makes a reference to it, and makes it in exactly the same illustrative fashion that Jesus Himself used,—' When Thou shalt make his soul a guilt-offering, he shall see his seed, he shall prolong his days, and the pleasure of the Lord shall prosper in his hand.' It is not likely that the writer of the great oracle reached his great discovery—that by suffering one man may save another—by studying the sacrificial ritual. He lived at the end of the Exile, and probably had never seen a Hebrew sacrifice offered. He had been poring over the fate of his people in Exile ; he had noticed that the best of them suffered most, just because they were the best ; and he, wondering why and why and why, had at last struck on the great truth that Israel—or the Remnant of Israel that was staunch, or perhaps only some one best Israelite—was suffering to save the nation, or even the nations. And he saw that the guilt-offering of the ritual of which he had heard would illustrate his discovery, so he used the illustration. Or, rather, he saw that behind the ritual there was a great truth, which it might teach—the truth that if the righteous enter into fellowship with the sinful, themselves remaining righteous, they may restore the sinful to the lost fellowship with God that is worship and life and bliss. [1]

I suggest that our Lord's references to ritual at the Supper were of a like kind. He used it for illustration ; yet there was something more. He saw the one unifying truth that lay behind the ritual. There have been different accounts of the original meaning of sacrifice. Some find it to be the giving of gifts to one's god, others the holding of fellowship with one's god. All add that, at a given stage in the evolution of religion, there emerged the idea that sacrifice might restore the covenant between

[1] There is an account of what I mean here in the chapter on ' The Atonement ' in *The Christian Experience* (chap. xv.).

a god and his devotees that had been broken by sin. After all, there is something common to the three accounts. It is fellowship. No one would give gifts to a god unless he were in fellowship with him, or wished to be. Again, the sin-offering and guilt-offering sought to restore a broken fellowship. By the end of the Old Testament period this idea was dominant. The older name for fellowship was ' covenant.' Israel was in covenant with Jehovah. Both ' burnt-offering ' and ' peace-offering ' said this in different ways. Sin interrupted this fellowship. ' Sin-offering ' and ' guilt-offering ' sought to renew the broken fellowship. The Passover, from its beginning, symbolized Jehovah's covenant with His people. It did not make the covenant, indeed, but took it for granted. The Day of Atonement symbolized both the devastating separation that sin works, and the renewal nevertheless of covenant. Sacrifice, like all other ritual, is a means of worship, and worship is fellowship with God.

It may seem to some that there is here a laboured exposition of a simple story. There are two answers. First, throughout the Synoptic Gospels, and particularly in their accounts of the Lord's Supper, we have only an incomplete account of what Jesus said. With inspired insight the Evangelists select the pivotal words, but they leave later generations to spell out the full meaning. Second, if an attempt be made to elucidate all that is implied in any conversation among old friends, especially on a memorable occasion, it will be found a long task. The comparatively few spoken words are laden with the wealthy implications of the intimacy of love. This phenomenon reaches its climax in the Last Supper.

If the exposition be correct, two currents of thought blent in Jesus' words. First, He set Himself to undo the disciples' sad conviction that their fellowship with Him had now an end. Next, He tried to show them once more that by suffering unto death He would fulfil the Law and the Prophets and be Messiah indeed ; but, according to His wont, He put the Prophets first.[1] And this appeal to the Old Testament was founded on fellowship. Indeed, we have reached the notion of fellowship by four different routes. First, we traced the use of the symbol of the common meal ; then we found a reference to the true way of fellowship in Jeremiah's prophecy of the New Covenant ; next we began a little to explore the deeps of the great oracle of the Suffering Servant, with its doctrine of salvation by fellowship ; lastly, we found that our Lord's sacrificial references, refusing to be applied to any single piece of ritual, all illustrate that idea of fellowship that lies behind all ritual. The Sacrament of the Lord's Supper is well called ' the Holy Communion,' for ' communion ' is just Latin for ' fellowship.'

The full statement of the Christian doctrine of fellowship would use the word thrice : We have fellowship with Christ and He with us ; so we have fellowship with God ; so, too, we have fellowship with each other. This is the burden of the wondrous chapters of the Fourth Gospel that occur just where the story of the institution of this Sacrament occurs in the Synoptic Gospels. Does not this coincidence confirm the interpretation of the Supper here put forward ? Jesus was telling the disciples that their old fellowship with Him was not to be broken, but, on the contrary, was now to be consummated. It was to be consummated because, through His entering on the Cross into full fellowship with sinful men, Himself remaining sinless, it would be possible for them to enter into full fellowship with Him.[2] They and He are one now as never before. ' I in them and Thou in Me, that they also may be in Us.' And the Lord's Supper is the symbol of all these truths, or, rather, of the one truth that is so

---

[1] Cf. Matt. xxvi. 56.　　　[2] See footnote on p. 154.

many-sided and means so much. When a Christian
partakes of the Lord's Supper, its simple symbols express
for him all this, and more also, and, in expressing, they
enhance the experience that they express. What is the
experience ? It is an experience of fellowship with Christ.
Once more, it is not a fellowship with an absentee. In
the Eucharist, Christ is present as really, as objectively,
as if He was there ' in the flesh.' Indeed, He is more
really present, for the spiritual surpasses the material,
and to know what this meaneth—' Christ in me, the hope
of glory '—is more than to ' lean on His breast at the
supper.'

D. The Pauline and Johannine Passages

Two passages in Paul's First Epistle to the Corinthians
and one in the Fourth Gospel need also to be studied.
We will begin with the Pauline passages, and take the
later of them first.

The passage 1 Cor. xi. 17–34 contains Paul's account of
the institution of the Supper. For the present purpose,
only four details need to be noticed. First, the words
' This do in remembrance of Me,' are added at one point,
and ' This do, as oft as ye drink it, in remembrance of
Me,' at another. These additions, whether original or
not, suit the circumstances of the early Church, as it
repeated the Supper, rather than of the Twelve as they
sat at the board with the living Jesus.[1] They bring out
the truth, about which Sacramentalist and Sacerdotalist
agree, that there is a commemorative aspect of the Lord's
Supper.

The second detail is this—instead of the words ' This
is My blood of the covenant,'[2] Paul has, ' This cup is the

[1] The first of them is found also in Luke xxii. 19 (though not in all ancient
authorities).   [2] Mark xiv. 24.

new covenant in My blood.' It seems to me that the change suggests that Paul interpreted the Supper symbolically and not literally, for no one would mean that a ' cup ' was literally a covenant. There is sure, however, to be divergence of opinion about such niceties of exegesis. The third detail is the use of the phrase, ' As often as ye eat this bread, and drink this cup, ye proclaim the Lord's death till He come.'[1] The force of the last three words will be discussed later. They seem clearly to mean that there is a sense in which Christ is not present at the Supper. The earlier words in the sentence show how closely Paul connected the Supper with the death of Christ. As I should say, they mean that in the Supper there is a symbolic representation of the way in which Christ, through His death, becomes one with men, and men with Him. The fourth detail is the most important for our immediate purpose. It is the use of the phrase, ' Whosoever shall eat the bread or drink the cup of the Lord unworthily shall be guilty of the body and the blood of the Lord.'[2] Can this strong phrase be taken symbolically? My answer is, ' Yes,' and I should sustain the answer by the considerations that lead me to a similar answer about certain phrases in the Tenth Chapter of the same Epistle, to which we now turn.[3]

First, there is a question of translation. The Greek of the New Testament has two sets of words to denote ' sharing.' In one group (κοινωνία, κτλ.) the fact emphasized is that *all* share, in the other (μετοχή, κτλ.) that *each* shares. The common translation for the noun in the first group is ' fellowship ' ; the best translation for the noun in the second is ' participation,' with the verb ' partake.' Words of both groups are found together in two passages.[4] The first passage shows that it is not easy always to translate Greek terms by

---

[1] 1 Cor. xi. 26.   [2] 1 Cor. xi. 27.   [3] 1 Cor. x. 1–22.
[4] Heb. ii. 14 ; 1 Cor. x. 16 f., 20 f.

the same English words, for modern English does not admit of ' fellows ' in the sense of ' sharers.' But it is unfortunate, I think, that the Revisers have forsaken the usual translation, ' fellowship,' in the second passage, in favour of ' communion.' There is no doubt that the prevalent New Testament concept of ' fellowship ' is of a fellowship of spirit. I should translate, therefore, ' The cup of blessing, which we bless, is it not a fellowship of the blood of Christ ? The loaf which we break, is it not a fellowship of the body of Christ ? Seeing that there is one loaf, we, who are many, are one body, for we all partake of the one loaf.' From the second occurrence of the word ' body,' it seems clear that here it refers to the Church, and not only to the Sacramental bread. As I have urged above, this seems to me to show that we are in the realm of symbol.[1] Again, while a literal loaf is, of course, meant, the ' one loaf ' is clearly taken as a symbol of the unity of the Church. And there is an earlier hint that Paul is here using the language of symbol. In the first verses of the Chapter, after the current Philonic manner, he takes the cloud and sea of the Exodus as symbol of Baptism, and the smitten rock of the Wilderness as symbol of the Lord's Supper. The threefold use of the word ' spiritual ' in the context requires this. Yet Paul does not use any such term as ' is like ' or ' stands for.' On the contrary, he says, ' They . . . *were all baptized* unto Moses in the cloud and in the sea,' and ' They drank of a spiritual rock that followed them, *and the rock was Christ.*' It is plain, here at least, that Paul is using the physical as symbol of the spiritual. May he not do so again later in the chapter ?

There is, however, another part of the passage to quote. To many Sacerdotalists it seems one of the strongest of all. It runs, ' But I say that the things which the Gentiles sacrifice, they sacrifice to demons and not to

[1] See p. 41 ff.

God : and I would not that ye should be sharers (κοινωνοὺς) with demons. Ye cannot drink the cup of the Lord, and the cup of demons : ye cannot partake (μετέχειν) of the table of the Lord, and the table of demons.' Can this passage also be taken symbolically? In the first place two other passages where relevant phrases occur may be quoted : ' Woe unto you, scribes and Pharisees, hypocrites ! for ye say . . . If we had been in the days of our fathers, we should not have been *sharers* (κοινωνοὶ) with them *in the blood of the prophets* '[1]; ' For we are become *partakers* (μέτοχοι) of Christ, if we hold fast the beginning of our confidence firm unto the end.'[2] These are symbolic passages, and they seem to approximate to the verses in Corinthians as closely as the difference in subject-matter admits. Or again, to turn from the mere words, is there not as vigorous a use of symbolism in the well-known passages from Hebrews, ' They crucify to themselves the Son of God afresh, and put Him to an open shame '; ' Of how much sorer punishment, think ye, shall he be judged worthy, who hath trodden under foot the Son of God, and hath counted the blood of the covenant, wherewith he was sanctified, an unholy thing? '[3] To-day another point must be taken. Some scholars suggest that here the Apostle is using both the terms and ideas of the Mystery Cults. It is true that the context has references to heathen customs, but to what heathen customs? Certainly not to the Mystery Cults. ' If one of them that believe not biddeth you to a feast, and ye are disposed to go, whatsoever is set before you, eat, asking no question for conscience' sake. But if any man say unto you, This hath been offered in sacrifice, eat not. . . .'[4] It is impossible that any one should be invited to the secret rites of a Mystery Cult in this casual way, for their initiates were more seclusive than the Freemasons.

---

[1] Matt. xxiii. 29 f.   [2] Heb. iii. 14.   [3] Heb. vi. 6, x. 29.   [4] 1 Cor. x. 27 f.

Pains were expressly taken to make sure that every one present was an initiate, and that every initiate knew what the ceremony was and meant. Again, sacrifices used in the Mysteries would not be ' sold in the shambles.' [1] Paul is referring to a much more frequent phenomenon. When a Corinthian ate meat, it might have been dedicated to some god. The association of meat-eating with sacrifice was very old. In ancient times every slain animal was hallowed. Apparently an animal might still be conventionally hallowed even by a butcher before he offered its flesh ' in the shambles.' Again, at a feast, a man might drink to some god as to-day one may drink a toast. Such customs often survive long after they have become perfunctory or formal. Let us suppose that a Corinthian host had dedicated his meat to Aphrodite, and a guest drank a cup in Apollo's name. They were now, says St. Paul, partakers with those two heathen demons. Did he mean that the Corinthians ate Aphrodite's flesh or drank Apollo's blood ? Whatever may have been the way of the Mystery Cults, there was no such notion attaching to the ordinary sacrifices of the Greeks, and it is with these that Paul draws his comparison. [2]

It is now possible to leave details and face the general position. Paul was an assiduous student of the Old Testament, which teaches so clearly that an outward rite is no guarantee of spiritual experience. He lived in the great age of Jewish symbolism. Like other Christians, he found something in the death of Christ that was beyond explanation. In the Tenth Chapter of First Corinthians he tries, like other intense believers, to express this by strongly symbolic language. In the Eleventh Chapter he is deeply moved because converts of his own treat carelessly and thoughtlessly the Sacrament that commemorates the death of Christ.

[1] 1 Cor. x. 25.   [2] For the Mystery Cults see also Appendix, 3.

L

The very symbols that ought to express their fellowship
betray their divisions ! Instead of nourishing their
spiritual experience, the Eucharist is the occasion of
their shame ! Paul falls into a passionate expostulation.
No one can read it without feeling the rise of temper as
he reads. Is it impossible or unlikely that in such a
passage such a man in such an age should speak symbolically without a cold-blooded ' is like ' or ' stands
for ' ? It would have been surprising if he had not.
He tells his converts that wantonly to mar the fellowship
of the Eucharist is to kill Christ over again ! It is to
be ' guilty of the body and blood of the Lord.' And
so it is.

There remains the Sixth Chapter of John. Here, as
in Chapter Three, it is difficult to decide how much is
Christ's own words and how much is the Evangelist's
exposition. But it seems to me that something in the
discourse is our Lord's own. One reason is that the
discourse, in its underlying ideas, presents a remarkable
parallel to a great Synoptic passage.[1] This parallel
cannot be fully drawn out here, but we may note that in
both Peter makes a representative confession of disciple-
ship[2] ; in both Jesus, being hailed as Messianic king,
goes on to say that He must die and rise again[3] ; in both
this is a hard saying to the disciples[4] ; in both Jesus
declares that it is the way to success[5] ; in both there is
the significant word ' stumbling-block.'[6]

Apart from this parallelism, however, there is much
in the Sixth of John that exactly suits the occasion
described in the context. When Jesus fed the five
thousand with the five loaves and two fishes, He worked

---

[1] Luke ix. 10 ff. This view requires, however, the bringing together of two
stories that Mark separates (Mark vi. 34 ff. ; viii. 27 ff.). Yet even in Mark,
almost on the occasion of the second story, Jesus Himself recalls the first
(Mark viii. 14 ff.).

[2] Luke ix. 20 ; John vi. 68.   [3] Luke ix. 22 ; John vi. 51, 62.

[4] Luke ix. 23 ff. ; cf. Mark viii. 32 ff. ; John vi. 60 f.

[5] Luke ix. 27 ; John vi. 54   [6] Matt. xvi. 23 ; John vi. 61.

a kind of miracle that was very uncommon with Him—
a miracle for a multitude. It is hard for us to conceive
how great His popularity would at once become, and how
urgent the crowd would be for the perpetual repetition
of the miracle. It was in vain that Jesus took refuge
first on the mountain and then on the sea. The insistent
people followed Him as men hurry to a new gold-field.
They would fain have made Him king *instanter* ![1] Probably in any age the majority of people would make any
man king who could and would give them free meals for
ever. This is what the crowd urged on Jesus. And,
Jews as they were, they had their biblical parallel ; they
quoted the story of the daily manna of the distant past.
So far the Johannine story is true to the context.

What was Jesus to do ? He had long ago faced and
settled the problem involved. One of His three distinctive
temptations was to turn stones into loaves. He had
replied, ' Man shall not live by bread alone.' In other
words, He was not content merely to seek for Himself
or for others what we call ' material prosperity.' He
wanted something more than to produce ' a well-fed
mankind.' He knew that the body is subordinate to
the soul, and He meant to keep it in its place. A Roman
poet of the age has told us how the Caesars debauched
the Roman people by giving them ' bread and the amphi-
theatre.' Jesus refused to give even the more innocent
of the two gifts again. He knew that even His disciples
would suffer by its repetition. There is here a great
instance of His parsimony in miracle. It is clear, I think,
what Jesus would say to the multitude, of course in His
own peerless way.

But what would that way be ? The First Gospel gives
us the answer. Once Jesus' disciples came to Him and
asked, ' Why teachest Thou them in parables ? ' And He
replied, ' Because the method sorts people out.' Of

[1] John vi. 15.

course, this is to epitomize a famous passage in the Thirteenth of Matthew. I cannot stay to justify it, but can only say that it seems to me a fair epitome. Jesus used parable because through it those who were in earnest about the deeper things of life, who 'had ears to hear,' would begin to understand His deep message,—while the rest, refusing to see, would grow blind; refusing to hear, would grow deaf ; refusing to understand, would come to be unable to do so. This is not at all our current account of the purpose of parable, but it is the Master's own. In His own time people found parables difficult, not easy. We find them easy because of the exposition of nineteen hundred years. It seems to me that Jesus used all His symbols as He said He used the chief of them, parables. In the Sixth of John, fronted by an urgent crowd, that is set upon bread and bread only, He begins to sort them out by using symbol. He takes their instance of the manna and says, ' I am the bread of life.' So far all agree that His speech is symbolic. He means that man has need of spiritual food, as well as ' daily bread,' and to hold fellowship with Him, to become one with Him—in symbolic phrase, to ' eat ' Him—is the way to satisfy that deeper need. The crowd at once begins to refuse this spiritual food. At the end of the chapter we find that a small band of disciples clings to Him—but for others this kind of teaching is only an ' occasion of stumbling.' When the crowd presses Him further, He reiterates His symbol, ' I am the living bread which came down out of heaven.'[1]

So far it seems to me quite possible that John's story is substantially true to the situation in question. The main difficulty is with the following paragraph.[2] Here three ways are open. Under the first the paragraph is referred to the same historical situation as the context. This suits best the Evangelical interpretation of its phrases, because,

[1] John vi. 51.
[2] John vi. 52-8, or, rather, from the middle of verse 51 (where ' flesh ' first occurs).

if they were spoken in the Galilean days, it is impossible that the first hearers should take them in the Sacerdotal sense. Yet I cannot persuade myself that this is the right way. Under the second way the paragraph (or a longer part of the chapter) is treated as one of the ' displacements ' of the Fourth Gospel, and is referred to the time of the Last Supper. This, too, seems to me unlikely, not least because the Fourth Evangelist already has a discourse for that occasion,[1] a discourse that interprets the Supper aright, though it is very different from the present paragraph. If, however, this account be accepted, it seems to me that its exposition would follow the same lines as under the third account. Under this the paragraph is an insertion by the Evangelist, in which he gives his own exposition of the meaning of Jesus' words to the crowd in the Capernaum Synagogue. This seems to me to be the most likely suggestion. It accords with the Evangelist's practice elsewhere (particularly in John iii. 16–21). The exposition given is the true one ; John does tell us what Jesus meant ; but his terms were suggested by phrases customary at the Lord's Supper in later days. In terminology, therefore, the paragraph is anachronistic, but not in meaning.[2]

Is there any support, outside the Fourth Gospel itself, for the symbolic exposition of this paragraph ? I myself think the symbolism unlikely to originate in a writer whose canons are Western[3] ; does it overpass the limits of Eastern symbolism, particularly in the period when the

---

[1] John xiii.–xvii.

[2] The general arguments against the exposition of early Christianity in terms of the Mystery Religions, referred to the Appendix (p. 216), seem to me to apply here. It is agreed that the Fourth Evangelist was a Jew ; could any Jew, whether Christian or not, bring himself to believe that he was eating God, or eating a god—whichever phrase be preferred ?

[3] Yet, when once it had originated in the East, multitudes of Western Christians, Evangelical to the core, have used without demur the Collect that includes the words, ' Grant us . . . so to eat the flesh of Thy dear Son, Jesus Christ, and to drink His blood. . . .' They have taken the words symbolically, and in using them have found the Lord present. I have already referred to the vivid symbolism of many Evangelical hymns (p. 142).

Gospel was written? To deal with this question fully would need a long examination of the literature of the first and second centuries, but there is one writer, in particular, whose trend of thought was in some ways much like the Fourth Evangelist's, and who consciously or subconsciously quotes from the Fourth Gospel in not a few passages. I mean Ignatius of Antioch. It may not be out of place, therefore, to quote some of his phrases, so as to show how far the use of metaphorical and symbolical language could go in the environment in which our Fourth Evangelist himself wrote.[1] Writing to the Ephesians, Ignatius speaks of them ' as being temple stones, made ready beforehand for a building of God the Father, being carried up to the heights through the engine [machine] of Jesus Christ, which is the cross, using the Holy Spirit as rope, and your faith being the thong, and your love the path [? inclined plane] that carrieth [you] up unto God.'[2] Again, wishing to say that, Ephesus being a stage on the way to Rome, the Ephesian Christians helped disciples passing to martyrdom at the capital, Ignatius writes, ' You are a passage [transit-path] for those who are being put to death unto God.'[3] To the Magnesians he speaks of ' The new leaven, which is Jesus.'[4] To the Trallians he says, ' Flee evil off-shoots that have brought forth deadly fruit, of which, if any taste, forthwith he dies. For these are not plants of the Father, for if they were, they would appear branches of the cross, and their fruit would be incorruptible.'[5] In his letter to the Romans, Ignatius has, again, two very remarkable symbolic passages— ' Suffer me to belong to the wild beasts, through whom it is [possible] to attain God. I am God's wheat, and I am

[1] I do not, of course, mean to suggest that I am discussing or quoting all that Ignatius says about the Eucharist. This belongs to the detailed history of the doctrine, which this Lecture does not pursue. I wish here only to illustrate the symbolical language of the time, and I have tried to choose indisputably symbolic passages.

[2] *Eph.* ix.   [3] *Eph.* xii.   [4] *Mag.* x.   [5] *Tralls.* xi.; cf. *Philad.* iii.

ground by wild beasts' teeth, in order that I may be found pure bread. Rather humour the beasts, that they may become a tomb for me'[1]; ' Living I write to you, longing to die. . . . I do not delight in the food of corruption nor pleasures of this life. I desire God's bread, which is the flesh of Christ, who is of David's seed, and I desire as drink His blood, which is incorruptible love. I wish to live no longer after the fashion of men.'[2] Lastly, to the Philadelphians, Ignatius says, 'Taking refuge in the gospel as the flesh of Jesus, and the Apostles as the eldership [presbytery] of the Church.'[3]

It seems to me to be clear from these passages that an even more extreme use of symbol was possible in the environment of the writer of the Fourth Gospel than his own in his Sixth Chapter or any other chapter. Further, it appears that, particularly when speaking of the death of Christ, Christian writers of that time might betake themselves to symbols and metaphors that seem to us strained. Again, it is clear that the metaphor and symbol of ' bread,' in particular, could be put to extreme uses, and to uses that furnish as near parallels to the paragraph in the Sixth of John as the differences in the context allow. Again, in the first of the passages from the Roman Epistle, Ignatius uses the eating of flesh as symbolic of the making of bread, and the latter as typical of fellowship with God ; it seems to me that John uses the eating of bread as symbolic of the eating of flesh, and the latter as typical of fellowship with God ; is the first line of thought possible, and the second impossible ? Finally, in the second quotation from the Roman Epistle, it is impossible to take literally the phrases, ' I desire God's bread, which is the flesh of Christ,' and ' I desire

---

[1] *Rom.* iv.

[2] *Rom.* vii. f.   Here, as noted below, the context requires that Ignatius' immediate reference is not to the Eucharist, but to the martyr's fellowship in Christ's Cross.

[3] *Philad.* v.

drink, His blood,' and to do justice to the context. What Ignatius is saying is not, ' I long for the Eucharist,' but ' I long for martyrdom.' The former would have no relevance at all to his plea with the Romans that they would not try to save him from the arena. On any interpretation, therefore, these phrases, which are so like those used at the institution and those used in the Sixth of John, must be taken symbolically, and not literally. Ignatius, desiring—as the context shows—to say that he longs to die as his Lord Himself died, and so to enter into a close fellowship with Him indeed, does so by using the familiar language of the Supper.[1] In other words, when he wished to speak of fellowship with Christ, he fell naturally upon the words of the great Sacrament of the Christian's fellowship with his Lord, and used them symbolically. Why, then, cannot the Johannine phrases be symbolic too? It seems to me that in this crucial paragraph[2] we have by implication a second account of this writer's exposition of the Eucharist, parallel to the exposition of chaps. xiii.–xvii., but symbolic in form—in the same form, that is, that our Lord Himself had used at Capernaum.

It only remains to add that there is a verse in the Sixth of John itself which seems to require that the passage is symbolic. Near its close there are the words, ' It is the spirit that quickeneth; the flesh profiteth nothing.'[3] It may be that the saying belongs to the Evangelist, and not to Jesus, though I do not think that ' the flesh ' here is exactly synonymous with ' My flesh ' in the previous verses, and our Lord uses a partly similar phrase in Mark.[4] But in any case does not the phrase make just that distinction between the outward and the inward so often named above, and assert that it is the inward that is essential in Christianity, not

---

[1] See Lightfoot's note on the passage.   [2] John vi. 52–8.
[3] John vi. 63.   [4] Mark xiv. 38.

the outward? I do not think that a writer who used the words 'flesh' and 'blood' literally in the preceding paragraph would have written or quoted this sentence. The Fourth Evangelist does not flatly contradict himself.

E. What is Distinctive in the Eucharist?

One of the questions that the Sacerdotalist presses upon the Sacramentalist is this: 'What, on your account, is distinctive, or peculiar, in the Eucharist? Is there anything in it that marks it off, for instance, from a Prayer Meeting or a Fellowship Meeting? For me there is something peculiar in the Eucharist; I believe that the very body and blood of our Lord are to be found in the elements of bread and wine; this is not true of any other of the "means of grace," not even of the Sacrament of Baptism. Do you think that the Eucharist is in any way unique? If so, in what way?' The question is a fair one. Before answering it, it will be well to look a little at the Sacerdotalist's own account of the *differentia*—if one may use the appropriate technical term—of the Lord's Supper. He undoubtedly does find something unique in the Eucharist. Neither he nor any one else claims that our Lord is present in any physical way in any other of the means of grace. What has the Sacramentalist to say of the claim?

The Sacramentalist has many objections to this account. Most of them are well known, and have been often urged. I make no attempt to state or discuss them exhaustively. I wish only to say some things about the Sacerdotalist definition of the *differentia* of the Lord's Supper from the point of view taken throughout this Lecture.

There is a postulate underlying the whole of the present discussion.[1] It is that in the universe that God has made

[1] See chap i. and Appendix, 1.

—and in all that He does—there is a certain quality of congruity or harmony or consistency. He does not deny Himself. I wish to urge this postulate against the Sacerdotalist account of the *differentia* of the Eucharist, and to do so in several particular ways.

First, this account seems to me inconsistent with the general teaching of Scripture about the relation of the outward and the inward, the material and the spiritual. In the third chapter I have tried to show what this teaching is. The claim that in the Eucharist there is a physical presence of Jesus, and that, *because* there is this physical presence, a blessing comes to those who are willing to receive it, seems to me directly to contravene this teaching. In other words, it introduces a disconsonance or disharmony into the universe of God. I need not labour this further.

Again, it seems to me that the belief that in the Eucharistic elements our Lord is physically present, makes the first Eucharist incongruous with all its later instances. The Sacramentalist has sometimes been shy of answering the question at the head of this section ; the Sacerdotalist has been as shy of answering another : ' How could our Lord's physical body and blood be present in the elements at the Institution of the Supper, as He Himself was sitting, body and blood, at the table? ' There have been several different answers to the question, but none really answers it. If I may say so reverently, it seems to me that, if our Lord held the Sacerdotalist opinion, He ought to have said, not ' This is My body,' ' This is My blood,' but ' When hereafter ye take bread in this way, that bread will be My body,' ' When hereafter ye take a cup in this way, its wine will be My blood.' This difficulty has, of course, often been urged, and I do not need to stress it further.

Again, the Sacerdotalist sometimes uses the term ' miracle ' of his account of the Eucharist, and adds that

miracles are inexplicable. It seems to me that the kind
of ' miracle ' that he finds in the Eucharist contradicts
the New Testament account of miracle, and does so in
two ways. First, this account requires that an out-worn
definition of ' miracle ' be accepted.[1] When the trans-
formation of the bread and wine into Christ's body and
blood is called a ' miracle,' this means that God does
something disconsonant with His universe. In no other
instance is it asserted that the senses belie the mind—
that a thing seems to the senses of sight and touch to be
one thing, while all the time it is also something else that
ought to respond to the tests of sight and touch, but does
not. In other words, the Sacerdotalist account of the
differentia of the Eucharist requires that God should
contradict Himself.

But there is also another way in which the Sacerdotalist
doctrine conflicts with the New Testament account of
miracle. There the significant name for a miracle is
a ' sign ' (σημεῖον). This name involves a certain
account of the wonders wrought by Christ and the
Apostles. This account is most explicit in the Fourth
Gospel, but it is by no means confined to that book.
Under it a miracle is never an end in itself. It is a wonder
that is meant to draw the mind to a spiritual truth. It
is a sign-post, not a goal. Now, it is required in sign-
posts that they be obvious. All the New Testament
miracles appeal to the evidence of the senses. For
instance, when the man ' sick of the palsy ' was ' borne
of four ' into Jesus' presence, He said to him two things :
' Thy sins are forgiven thee ' and ' Rise, take up thy bed
and walk.' And the sick man rose and did so. And
Jesus explicitly appealed to this obvious, sensible phenomenon as token of something deeper and spiritual. It
would have been no use to say, ' This man still looks like
a paralytic, but he is really healed—and so you must

---

[1] See Appendix, 1.

believe that the Son of Man hath power on earth to forgive sins.' A New Testament miracle, if it is to be a miracle, must be obvious to the senses. Here, therefore, the claim that in the Eucharist there is a repeated ' miracle ' is incongruous with the New Testament account of miracle. This too has often been urged, and I need not pursue it further.

It seems to me, finally, that the Sacerdotalist opinion is inconsistent with the Christian doctrine of the Incarnation. That doctrine, of course, is that our Lord Jesus Christ is both God and man, or—lest this phrase should seem to make His person twofold—that He is the God-Man. In order to make my meaning clear it is necessary to recall the relation that the personal or spiritual, in God and man respectively, bears to the outward or material.

Usually theology has distinguished two relations of God to the world of nature or of things. They have been called creation and providence, or, better, transcendence and immanence. The first term denotes the distinction or separateness of God from the world, together with the notion that it is dependent for existence and worth upon His will. The Sacerdotalist doctrine of the Real Presence does not attach itself to this concept. The second term, immanence, denotes the idea that God is present and operative in and through all His universe, without becoming part of it—without submitting to spatial or temporal or material conditions. Some modern expositions relate this doctrine to that of the Holy Spirit. In older days Christian thinkers did not usually go so far. They taught, indeed, that the Spirit of Christ dwells in Christian men, and in the Christian Church. Sometimes they went on to claim that He ' strives with ' men who have not yet become Christian, and thereby is in a limited way present in their lives. But they did not usually go on to assert that the Spirit of God dwells also

in nature, and they did not use the term ' immanence '
much at all. To-day the tendency of Christian thought
is to find the Holy Spirit immanent in every part of the
universe, and not only in man. It needs to go on,
however—it is already going on—to point out that the
term ' immanence ' varies in meaning according to the
nature of the creature in question—that immanence
means one thing when used of man, another when used
of animals, another when used of stones, and so on.
In other words, we are coming to see that there are
different species or kinds of immanence, yet that the one
Spirit of God is operative in all, and that the culminant
instance is the indwelling of the Spirit in Christian men.
I have already said that this is one of the places where
the unity of the Son and the Spirit—and not their distinction—appears. ' Christ in you ' and the indwelling Spirit
are one and the same.

Christian theology adds no third to these two ways of
relating God to the world of nature or ' matter.' Under
both it says emphatically ' God is Spirit ' and not material.
In other words, it denies that God can have a body. It
is not, then, as divine that Jesus' body and blood are
found in the Eucharist.

The relation of man to the material world is different.
Man, unlike God, is body and spirit or soul, or, if it
be preferred, body-soul. A given part of the material
universe, called his body, is part of him. Not only so,
but through his body he reaches the rest of the world of
nature, and is in turn reached by it. Through the eye
he sees, through the ear he hears, and so on. When the
Nicene Creed says that God the Son ' became man,' it
means that He took such a body as men have. It means,
as I think, more than this, but it does mean this. In the
Incarnation the Christian doctrine both of God and man
culminates. The Old Testament had reached the conclusion ' Man is made in the image of God ' ; the New adds

that God both could and did become man. And, becoming man, the Incarnate Son is for ever the typical man, the representative man. What He is as man, other men ought to be. This seems to me to be one of the implications of Jesus' own chosen name, ' Son of Man.' Whatever be the origin of the phrase, His own words require that it meant this for Him and so for us.

Christian thought, led by Paul, has carried this comparison into the Hereafter. In the Fifteenth of First Corinthians, in particular, Paul argues that the Risen Christ has a ' body,' and that therefore we too shall have ' bodies ' in Eternity. He says, also, that they will be both like and unlike our bodies here—just as our Lord's risen body was both like and unlike His body here. For Paul the risen Jesus is still the typical man. What He is as man, we are to be. The ' body of His glory ' is the type of ours. For myself, I accept this teaching. I ' believe in the resurrection of the body.' This is not the place to argue this opinion.[1] The important point here is that Paul refers to it in his account of the Institution of the Lord's Supper. He says, ' We do show forth the Lord's death *until He come.*' As man our Lord now has a body, and the day will come when ' He shall be made manifest.' He is still incarnate. This is asserted by many Sacerdotalists. It seems to me that it gives a true account of our Lord's relation to the material world as man. It means, however, that as incarnate He is now absent. Else there could be no Parousia. It is not, therefore, as human that His physical presence can be claimed in the Eucharist. But if that presence is consonant neither with His divinity nor His humanity, with what in Him is it consonant ? Is there a third element in His nature ?

There are, however, to-day many Christians who do not believe in a physical resurrection. They believe in the

[1] Something is said of it in *The Christian Experience,* chap. xxiv.

survival of the soul, but not in the 'resurrection of the body,' in however carefully defined a sense. So far as I understand them, they hold that men will survive as finite spirits, each with his own personality intact. They are not pantheists, resolving all finite spirits into the one great Spirit. I suppose they hold, too, that Jesus Christ, considered as human, is the type of what those spirits will be. They do not add, however, that for other men there is to be a relation to the physical world analogous to that postulated by Sacerdotalists for our Lord in the Eucharist. In other words, on this account of the Hereafter also, the Sacerdotalist opinion is disconsonant with the humanity of the Living Christ. It is not as man that He is held to be physically present in the Eucharist. So we reach the same question as before. If the assertion of the Physical Presence is not consonant with that which is divine in His nature, nor with that which is human, where is there any room for it in the doctrine of His person ?

In these last paragraphs I have, of course, been traversing certain phrases current among Sacerdotalists. Some of them like to speak of their Eucharistic doctrine as the 'extension of the Incarnation,' and the adjective 'Incarnational' has been coined to denote it. I have implicitly been asking that they should tell us more exactly what they mean by these phrases, and in particular that they should relate them more clearly to the great doctrine of the Incarnation. The New Testament would, as it seems to me, allow the phrase 'the extension of the Incarnation' in two senses, but not in a third. Under the first it might be applied to the doctrine of the Spirit of Christ. As St. John puts it, 'I will send you another Paraclete, that He may be with you for ever.' As it has been recently put, 'the Spirit is Jesus back again.' This seems to me the less suitable of the two possible uses of the phrase. Under the more suitable, the 'extension of the Incarnation' would mean that Jesus is

incarnate still, and will always be incarnate. But this
links with the doctrine of the Resurrection, not with that
of the Eucharist. And here we reach a place where the
distinction between the Son and the Spirit is exemplified.
As more than once stated already, I think that for the
period between the Ascension of Christ and His Parousia
the *unity* of the Son and the Holy Spirit is for us the
operative side of the truth ; for the days when the Son
was alive in Palestine, and for the consummation that
begins with the Parousia, it seems to me that their
distinction is for us the operative side of the truth.
Christian theology, that is, requires both their unity and
difference. But there seems to me to be no room for the
doctrine of the Physical Presence within its limits. The
word ' Incarnational ' would apply quite well to the
doctrine that there is a place for a ' body ' in the Hereafter for Christ and so for other men. To apply it to the
relation of God to the universe seems to me to confuse
it with ' immanental.'

Before trying to answer the question, ' What is the
differentia of the Eucharist on the Sacramental account
of it ?,' I must premise a remark already made.[1] Difference is not incompatible with likeness. Every rose has its
own difference, yet every rose belongs to the class ' roses '
—that is, it is like other roses. Every man has his own
' individuality '—or, to use a more exact word, and to
use it in its proper sense, his own idiosyncrasy—yet he is
like other men as well as different from them. Everest is
unique among the Himalayas, yet it is part of the range.
Similarly, while the Lord's Supper has its own distinction
among symbols, it is yet like them. Its relation to them
is not one of incongruity. To compare it with other
means of grace is like comparing different mountains, not
like comparing a mountain with a star. To take the
world of Christian symbols—which is a narrower world

[1] See p. 109.

than that of the means of grace—even within it the
Eucharist is a climax rather than an exception. In other
words the Sacramentalist recognizes the likenesses of
the Eucharist to other means of grace, as well as its
distinction from them. Probably the Sacerdotalist will
admit the claim here made, and even assert it. Perhaps,
then, I may be allowed to put the variety of opinion in
this way : the Sacerdotalist counts the distinction of the
Eucharist of more moment than its likeness to other
means of grace ; the Sacramentalist or Evangelical
counts the likeness of more importance than the difference.
He would say, for instance, that Christ was as fully
present in the first Christian prayer-meeting of which we
have any detail[1] as in the Eucharist.

But what is the Sacramentalist account of the *differentia*
of the Eucharist ? The answer has been already given,
in large part, in the first section of the chapter on
Baptism, but it is perhaps well to recapitulate. The
first distinctive fact about the Eucharist is that, like the
Sacrament of Baptism, and like that alone, it has the
authority of our Lord Himself. He appointed these two,
and no other, of the symbols of the Church, and this
gives to them a unique obligation. There are some
Christians who deny that our Lord intended them to be
repeated, and others who claim that they were not
instituted by our Lord at all. I am not here speaking of
them, but of those who agree that Jesus Christ Himself
instituted the two Sacraments and directed His people
to observe them ' till He come.' For such Christians,
I say once more, these Sacraments are obligatory as no
other symbol can ever be. Can the neglect of them be
called anything less than sin ?

But the Eucharist is the climax of symbolism, not
only because our Lord Himself instituted it, but because
of its nature. In the second and fourth chapters we saw

[1] Acts iv. 23 ff.

M

that in all human life a special emphasis falls on symbols of covenant—or, if a deeper word be preferred, on symbols of fellowship. Examples were taken from marriage, treaties, and so on. If symbols of covenant among men are pre-eminent, how much more shall symbols of covenant with God be! If the Himalayas are supreme among mountains, Everest is supreme among the Himalayas.

As noted in chapter four, this characteristic leads to another.[1] It is so important that I venture to state it again almost in the words in which I stated it some years ago,[2]—'It may be said that in every act of Christian worship—praise, prayer, intercession, vow, sermon—Christ is present, and that therefore for the Evangelical the Sacrament has no *differentia* among means of grace. Is it not true, indeed, of a sincere Christian that Christ is with him always—in his daily work, in his home, in his leisure, as well as in his worship? What, then, is there distinctive in the Eucharist? Part of the answer may perhaps be made out if a certain law of all human fellowship be remembered : *Fellowship is usually assumed but occasionally asserted.* For instance, when two friends talk, they are continuously using their fellowship, though they directly attend, not to it, but to something else—a coming holiday, say, or some " business " problem. They assume the fact of fellowship. But just for two moments, when they meet and when they part, they assert it by the hand-grip. For one to refuse the other that hand-grip would mean the end of their fellowship. So too the life of home, feeding on fellowship, usually takes it for granted. A thousand other things absorb immediate attention, a hundred problems are solved in common. The fellowship through which they are solved may not once be named, yet it is the necessary postulate of the common life. It is un-named, yet

---

[1] See pp. 109 f.

[2] In an article on ' The Real Presence,' in *The Interpreter* for January 1918.

without it home would perish. Still, there do come times when it is asserted. As the birthday of each member of the home comes, the other members bring the precious tokens of communion, saying, " We love you." Again, do we not sometimes hear of women in middle-life who say, " I know my husband loves me as dearly as ever ; our whole life builds on that ; and there is sometimes the kiss or the caress ; but I wish it were oftener. I could better face the hardships of our common life so " ? Or, again, did not Dr. Dale, speaking once of his church in England to an Australian audience, say, " I know they love me, but they do not often tell me so " ? His heart yearned for the direct sign of the constant fellowship. And, when he came home, his church, having somehow heard of the saying, greeted him with a symbol of its love. Fellowship, to be effective, needs both continuous assumption and occasional assertion.

' It will have been noticed that the assertion is always by symbol. The hand-grip, the birthday gift, the kiss, are all " outward and visible signs." As fellowship is itself something spiritual, and so unseen, this *must* be so. Fellowship may be manifested in many ways, but it can *only* be *asserted* by symbol. The application to the Lord's Supper is simple. In his workaday life the true Christian does hold constant fellowship with his Lord, but there it is one of the things that he takes for granted. He must needs attend directly to a thousand other things. A psychologist would call this kind of fellowship " sub-conscious." In its degree this is even true of all " means of grace " except the Sacraments.[1] When we listen to a sermon, when we hold fellowship with each other about the things of God, even when we speak directly to Christ

[1] In the Sacrament of Baptism there is the assertion of the presence of God the Holy Spirit.

in hymn or prayer, we rather take our fellowship with Him for granted than assert it. We attend primarily to something else. We are nearer the express assertion than when we are about "secular" work, but we do not quite reach it. A parallel may again be drawn from home. When a home's members are scattered about their daily work, their fellowship does not lapse. It underlies their whole life all the time. When they gather together in the evening and talk, the fact of fellowship draws nearer the centre of attention, yet attention does not rest on it, for they speak to each other of other things. Even if they directly praise or blame each other, their fellowship is still, to change the figure, the ground on which they stand rather than the thing at which they look But when the birthday gift comes, or the more frequent kiss, then the fellowship itself wins direct attention, and through direct attention renewal. The Christian's fellowship with Christ has three similar phases. It underlies his life " in the world " ; it is more prominent, though it is not more real, when he intercedes or praises or adores ; but it itself becomes the centre of thought, and so finds renewal, in the Lord's Supper. Such a direct assertion and renewal of fellowship is of peculiar value when the fellowship is with an *unseen* Friend. Every Christian knows how hard it is always to be aware of Christ's presence. He will therefore the more value the Sacrament that centres in the express assertion " Christ is here." The longing of Christian soldiers to partake of the Lord's Supper on the eve of battle is a poignant instance. They knew that directly to assert Christ's companionship on the night before they took part in an attack would make it easier to take His presence with them for granted when they " went over the top." In a Christian's communion with his Lord this Sacrament is what the kiss is in the fellowship of home.'

Finally, it seems to me that the Eucharist is the supreme symbol of the fellowship of the Church. It is not primarily meant for the ' outsider,' though it may sometimes preach him a sermon. It is primarily meant for the Christian community, and for the Christian individual. The account given above of the first Eucharist laid stress just on this point. It seems to me that similar stress should always be laid. In the Sacrament of the Lord's Supper, Christians—asserting their fellowship with their Lord, finding Him really present, feeding their fellowship with Him by the use of symbol—assert thereby their fellowship with each other, and nourish that fellowship too in a culminant way. Nor only their fellowship with the others who kneel at the same table, but with all Christians, past, present, future, as well. It is perhaps remarkable that, while one of the historic Creeds of Christendom names the Sacrament of Baptism, neither names the Eucharist directly. It is true, however, that, in an exposition of the Eucharist, all that is said after the words, ' I believe in the Holy Ghost,' whether in the Apostles' Creed or the Nicene, might be included. Indeed, I do not know whether a complete exposition of the Eucharist would not involve every article in the Creeds ! So wealthy a symbol is this ! But, to narrow the discussion again, it seems to me that the Eucharist exemplifies, more adequately than any other symbol, what is meant by ' the Communion of Saints.' Evangelicals have too often ignored this article of their faith. In the Sacrament of the Lord's Supper there is symbolized a fellowship with Christ, and therefore a fellowship with every Christian, of whatever clime or era. In it past, present, and future blend. Nor is this fellowship only pictured or imagined. To Christ every saint is ' really ' present. I should myself so interpret ' eternity ' as to assert this even of the Christians of the future. And, when Christians enjoy fellowship with Christ, they thereby enter into ' real ' fellowship with all the saints of all the ages. ' I believe in the Communion of Saints.' The Eucharist is *the* symbol that there is a Church. And, once more, there is no such thing as ' mere symbol.'

Here, O my Lord, I see Thee face to face.

ADDITIONAL NOTE ON 1 COR. V. 7 f. AND HEB. XIII. 9–15.

There are two other passages that are often quoted by Sacerdotalists in support of their doctrine of the Eucharist.[1] I have not named them above because I do not think that they refer to the Eucharist at all, but I ought perhaps to state briefly what I take them to mean. They both use allusions to the sacrificial ritual of the Old Testament. It is necessary first to recall the general nature of such allusions in the New Testament.

I have tried to show above that when our Lord referred to the sacrificial ritual at the Supper, He alluded to such parts of it as illustrated His meaning, choosing freely from different parts of it. He did not, for instance, confine Himself to the Passover, which was to be celebrated the next day. And, in referring to different pieces of ritual, He left on one side all the many details that did not illustrate His meaning. He omitted far more than He quoted, as any one will at once see who compares His references with the ritual itself. His use of the ritual, in other words, was purely illustrative. It was not the starting-point of His thought, but helped to elucidate it.

It seems to me that this is the general way of the New

[1] 1 Cor. v. 7 f. ; Heb. xiii. 9 ff.

Testament writers. It is followed, I think, even in the
Epistle to the Hebrews, which may at first seem an
exception. The writer draws a parallel, for instance,
between Jesus and Melchizedek. No one will suggest
that here the two passages about the ancient Priest-King
of Salem were the starting-point of thought. On the
contrary, the writer had certain convictions about
Jesus ; searching the Old Testament, he found that
Melchizedek illustrated them. Again, Jesus, the true
High-Priest, is said to fulfil the ritual of the Day
of Atonement ; but is He said to fulfil it all ?
Where, for instance, is there any reference to what
the Authorized Version wrongly calls the ' scapegoat ' ?
And why does the writer introduce a reference to ' the
ashes of an heifer,' which had nothing to do with the Day
of Atonement ? He selects such details as suit his purpose
and omits the rest. Of course, he urges that in the Jewish
ritual there were adumbrations of religious truths that
were perfectly manifested in Christ, but his way of showing
this is selective and illustrative. He did not really work
from the ritual to Jesus, but vice versa.

This is clearer still in the other New Testament writers.
For instance, when Paul writes ' Present your bodies a
living sacrifice unto God,'[1] or ' that the offering up of the
Gentiles might be acceptable,'[2] or ' I am poured out on the
sacrifice of your faith,'[3] or when the seer of the Apocalypse says, ' I saw underneath the altar the souls of ' the
martyrs,[4] the references to Hebrew ritual are merely
illustrative. To pass to examples nearer our subject,
when Peter compares the Christian Church to the Jewish
' priesthood,'[5] or the Apocalypse says that Christ has
made Christians to be ' priests to God,'[6] the meaning is
that there is a way in which every Christian is like an Old
Testament priest—namely, in having direct and personal

[1] Rom. xii. 1.   [2] Rom. xv. 16.   [3] Phil. ii. 17.
[4] Rev. iv. 9.   [5] 1 Pet. ii. 5, 9.   [6] Rev. i. 6, v. 10.

access to God. The general rule emerges that New
Testament allusions to the Old Testament ritual of
sacrifice are illustrative. It hardly needs adding that the
thing illustrated is to be discovered in each case from the
context. An examination of the passages just quoted
shows that there is no presumption whatever that an
allusion to sacrifice, as such, implies a reference to the
Lord's Supper.

The passage in the First Epistle to the Corinthians
runs as follows : ' Purge out the old leaven. . . . For our
Passover also hath been sacrificed, even Christ ; wherefore
let us keep festival, not with old leaven, neither with the
leaven of malice and wickedness, but with the unleavened
bread of sincerity and truth.' It seems to me that
this passage, too, exemplifies the rule stated. Paul is
inveighing against the Corinthians' toleration of incest.
He wants to tell them that true Christianity is inevitably
moral, and that therefore, if they be Christians, they
cannot tolerate sin in any one of the members of the
Church, else it will contaminate them. It strikes him
that he can illustrate this by the effect of leaven on a
' lump ' of dough. This suggests the Feast of Unleavened
Bread, which, in the first century, had long been one
with the Passover. He ' spiritualizes ' the custom of
putting away leaven at that feast. He selects a piece of
ritual that illustrates his meaning. Perhaps the metaphor
was all the more apposite because the feast was imminent.
Having ' spiritualized ' one thing in the feast, he
' spiritualizes ' another. ' Remember,' he says, ' that *we*
keep Passover, that *we* have a Passover Lamb—Christ.
Remembering *that*, surely we cannot tolerate sin.' From
the way in which he introduces the phrase ' Christ, our
Passover, was sacrificed (aorist),' it is likely that the
comparison of Christ with the Passover Lamb was
already common among Christians. But the comparison
is between the Crucifixion and the sacrifice of the Lamb

in the Temple, not between the subsequent eating of the
Lamb and the eating of the bread in the Eucharist.
' We keep festival,' says Paul, 'not by putting away leaven,
but by putting away sin, and this we can do because
Christ died.' The last clause is an exposition, but it is
the exposition that Paul's uniform teaching about the
Cross warrants, and it suits the context. The Apostle's
meaning is that Christians ' keep festival,' not ritually, but
by living a spiritual, and so a moral, life.

The passage in Hebrews runs, ' We have an altar,
whereof they have no right to eat which serve the taber-
nacle. For the bodies of those beasts, whose blood is
brought into the holy place [as an offering] for sin, are
burned without the camp. Wherefore Jesus also, that
He might sanctify the people through His own blood,
suffered without the gate. Let us therefore go forth
with Him without the camp, bearing His reproach.' Here
the writer is, for the last time, urging his readers to stand
firm in Christianity, even though they are therefore
ostracized by Judaism. He lays hold of a piece of the
old ritual that will illustrate and point his appeal. Here,
however, there is rather a contrast than a comparison—
a contrast with the ritual, but a comparison with the
Christ. The writer is set upon encouraging his readers to
suffer, as their leaders have already done,[1] for Christ's
sake. The particular suffering that falls to them is exclu-
sion from Judaism. This the writer compares to the
burning of the bodies of the sin-offerings, on the great Day
of Atonement, ' without the camp.' The spot where this
was done was no ' altar ' to a Jew, but an accursed
place. ' For us, however,' says this writer boldly, ' it is
an altar—it is our own peculiar altar, in which other Jews
have no part. We are outcast of our own people, as
Jesus Himself was, victims as He was, sacrifices as He
was.' The ' altar ' is the Cross. To ' eat ' of it is to suffer

[1] Heb. xiii. 7.

with Christ. The Hebrew Christian was called to 'drink of' His 'cup.' The writer is putting in one phrase what Paul put in two—' Christ redeemed us from the curse of the Law, having become a curse for us,' and ' I fill up on my part that which is lacking of the afflictions of Christ.'[1] Neither the passage itself, nor the context, seems to me to require or suggest any reference to the Eucharist.

[1] Gal. iii. 13 ; Col. i. 24.

VI

MEMBERSHIP, INTER-COMMUNION, AND REUNION

A. INTRODUCTORY

IN current discussion there are three other questions that touch the place of Sacraments and symbols in the life of the Church. The first is, Who shall be counted a member of the Church? The second is, Since there are to-day many separate churches—if that convenient plural may be used for the several parts of the one Church—under what rule shall one of these churches practise inter-communion with another? The third is, Shall the various churches seek reunion? The answers to these questions have historically involved, and still in practice involve, the problem of the right use of symbols. To all three the general answer follows from the discussions of the previous chapters. The threefold distinction made in the third chapter needs especially to be recalled. There it was seen that there are three elements in the religious life, named respectively the spiritual, the moral, and the ritual or symbolic. It was also seen that these three bear a given relation to each other—that the first is essential and primal, the second essential but derivative, while about the third the two truths were elucidated that it is indispensable in some form, and serviceable indeed, but that no particular form of it is essential to religion. It is from this point that the discussion of this chapter starts.

The first question, ' Who shall be counted a member

of the Church ? ' may conveniently be taken in two parts
—' What place have ritual and Sacrament in the *admission*
of members to the Church ? '[1] and ' What place have
ritual and Sacrament in the recognition of members as
continuing in the Church ? '[2] Here, of course, the subject
of the two Sacraments, Baptism and the Eucharist,
recurs. The other two questions—' Under what rule
shall churches practise inter-communion ? ' and ' Shall
the churches seek reunion ? '—may conveniently be
taken together.[3] In each instance, of course, the many
questions involved are only discussed in relation to
symbol and Sacrament.

B. Admission to the Church

The answer to the question, ' Who shall be admitted
to the Church ? ' has already been implicitly given.
Indeed, if the third and fourth chapters be taken together
it has been explicitly given. If an adult seeks the
membership of the Church, it is necessary to have some
proof that he knows what he is doing, and that he comes
from a sincere motive. To secure these ends in heathen
lands, missionaries usually interpose a period of instruc-
tion and test between the request for Baptism and
Baptism itself. In other words, they seek to discover
whether the inquirer has at least a desire to ' know God,
and Jesus Christ whom He has sent,' and whether this
desire has begun to show itself in its inevitable fruit, a
moral life. They look for the spiritual and moral elements
in the Christian life. If these are there, they add the
third, the symbol and Sacrament of Baptism. As has
already been shown, where this is rightly used, it not only
expresses an experience, but nourishes it. Here the
place of symbol in admitting a new member to the

[1] Section *B*.   [2] Section *C*.   [3] Section *D*.

Christian Church seems to the Evangelical peculiarly clear. To use a metaphor that has been a favourite with many, Baptism is here a ' seal,' serving both to express something that is past, something that is present, and something that is to last into the future.

Again as already stated, it seems to me that in Christian lands Baptism, the symbol of admission to the Church, ought to be administered to infants, if there is reasonable guarantee that the society called the Church—whether through the parents, or, in extraordinary cases, by other means—will fulfil the promise that falls to it in that Sacrament. I should maintain that the experience of fellowship with God has already begun for the child, even though he himself does not know it. Yet it also seems to me that this experience is so incipient and incomplete that some other symbol ought to be added when the child is able to take his own willing part in the fellowship. This symbol might either be the laying on of hands or the giving of the right hand of fellowship. When it is used, it means that, by the confession of the child himself, he does at least desire to know God in Christ, and that the Church is satisfied, by the beginnings of the fruit of such desire in the distinctively Christian kind of moral behaviour, that this desire is really his. It seems to me that this symbol, while it is complementary to Baptism, may, like the symbol of Baptism itself when used for adults, not only express, but nourish, that Christian experience that is fundamental to the Christian life. So much follows from what has already been said. It follows also that any church that holds such convictions should require its Ministers, not only to administer the Sacrament of Baptism, but to teach its obligatoriness and every other truth about it.

But other questions remain. Shall a church require an explicit belief in this Sacrament, not only from its *Ministers*, but also from every one of its *members* ? Shall

it exclude from membership a believer who, having
honestly reached the conclusion that no one ought to be
baptized until he is old enough to choose for himself,
declines to bring his children to Baptism? Shall it
exclude from membership any one who sincerely holds,
as do the Quakers and not a few modern scholars who
are not Quakers, that our Lord did not Himself institute
Baptism, and that this Apostolic practice is not perpetually binding on Christians? Shall the acceptance
or rejection even of this great symbol be a ' test of
membership ' in a church? Cannot the church practise
a greater catholicity in membership than in Ministry?
Ought it not to do so?

Historically the answer of the Methodist Church has
been, ' We will not refuse membership to a Christian
who sincerely holds either the Baptist or the Quaker
conviction.' I do not mean that the Methodist Church
has ever explicitly said this, but that this has been its
practice. It is well known that in the ' Rules of the
Methodist Societies,' drawn up by the two Wesleys, there
is no mention of Baptism at all. It is true, of course,
that these rules were intended as rules of membership in
certain ' Societies ' and not in the Church. There is no
doubt that Charles Wesley, at least, would have required
Baptism for membership in the Church. I think that
John Wesley would have done so too. There is no need,
however, to inquire here whether John Wesley held one
and the same doctrine on this subject throughout his life.
It seems to me that John Wesley, setting himself to
found a ' Society,' was unawares founding a church—
the word ' church ' again being used of a part of the one
Church, whose only founder is Jesus Christ. And it
seems to me that, just as in general John Wesley was,
in the purpose of God, doing more than he meant or
knew, so in the particular that he omitted to mention
Baptism in the Rules for his Societies he was following

the guidance of Christ. For the ultimate question is not ' Whom shall a church admit to membership ? ' but ' Whom does Jesus Christ accept as members ? ' The answer to the second question should be normative for the answer to the first. There are, of course, those who say that a given church is justified in rejecting some whom the Christ accepts, inasmuch as they may seek membership in other churches. Here is another question that it would be out of place fully to argue in this Lecture. But it will be noticed that this answer presupposes that there are several different churches of Christ in one place, and even that there ought to be several. I cannot admit this. I think that schism, however justifiable sometimes, is yet a mark of imperfection, and that every Christian church, in whatever ways it honestly can, ought to seek to do away with schism. It follows that, as the Church ought to be universal, it ought to seek to include every one whom Christ Himself accepts. Does He accept a man who sincerely holds Baptist or Quaker convictions ? The answer surely is, ' Yes, if that man lives in fellowship with Him, and if there is evidence of this in a consistent Christian behaviour.' Can any one deny that many a Baptist and Quaker has enjoyed this experience, and evidenced it in his daily ' conversation ' ? Of course, no one can. This being so, I hold that the consequences of the discussion above ought to be accepted. The primary and ' architectonic ' element in the Christian religion is a spiritual experience ; it is admitted that the man in question may have this, that he may be a true ' believer,' a real Christian. Again, it was seen above that this kind of spiritual experience will inevitably show itself in a given kind of behaviour that may be called distinctively ' the Christian life ' ; it is admitted that this, too, is found in many a man who holds the convictions in question. Thirdly, it was claimed that while such an experience will certainly show itself in some outward ' form ' or ritual or symbol or Sacrament, no particular form or ritual or symbol or Sacrament is essential. Finally, it was seen that the two Sacraments —the term being now used in the narrowest and highest sense—are authoritative or obligatory, not essential, for Christians. The Christians in question deny their obligatoriness. Shall this exclude them from a church that proclaims it ? I think that Methodism has been right in practising the answer ' No,' and it seems to me time that it should give the answer ' No ' outright. If we believe, to use an old phrase, that Quakers and Baptists ' go to heaven,' this seems to me the only reasonable thing to do. And, to refer again to the history of Methodism, has not our Church been happily free from controversy on this subject just because we have not tried to coerce individual practice ? In the ultimate issue, indeed, it is impossible to enforce a Sacrament. The phrase is a contradiction in terms. The way to secure the loyal practice of a Sacrament is to explain it, to enjoin it, and so to practise it among willing members that it shall commend itself to the unwilling. If and when the Sacerdotalist interpretation is universally repudiated, I think the number of those who refuse Baptism will dwindle, and even disappear. Meanwhile, to admit even a single unbaptized member into a church is to proclaim, by a not inappropriate symbol, that not even the Sacrament of Baptism is essential to salvation. The essential admits of no exceptions, but the obligatory may.

C. Continuance in the Church

We come now to the second of the three questions named at the beginning of the chapter : ' Who shall be reckoned as continuing in the membership of the Church ? ' I have stated above that it seems to me that in the answer to this question there is a place for the symbolic, and that our Lord Himself has decided what symbol shall fill that place. I cannot but agree with those who think that He instituted the Sacrament of the Lord's Supper, that He meant it to be perpetual in His Church, and that therefore it is obligatory upon all Christians. It follows, I think, that it ought to be required in the Ministers of a church, as the organs of its convictions, that they should declare their acceptance of these doctrines, and undertake loyally to practise and preach them. I may be asked whether I do not admit that there have been and are true Ministers of Christ who honestly deny these truths, and whether there ought not to be a place in a church of catholic mind for their Ministry. My answer is, ' No ; it seems to me that there are subjects on which the Ministers of a church ought to express its convictions, and that this is such a subject.' The grounds of this reply, again, cannot be laid out here.

If, however, Ministers are to express the convictions of churches, it does, I fear, follow, that there is as yet no possibility of the complete healing of the schisms of the Church. If all unjustifiable schisms were undone, there would yet remain three churches—the Sacerdotalist, holding that certain symbols are essential to the Church ; the Sacramental, holding that the two Sacraments are obligatory, that other symbols are serviceable, but that no symbol is essential ; and a third church, consisting of those who, denying that any symbol or Sacrament is either obligatory or essential, and looking upon all ritual as a hindrance rather than a help, strive to use it as little as possible. I do not at present see any way to heal these divisions. But may God, who is wiser than us all, quickly show us the way. And, in order that this may be so, may we all be humble enough to ' consider it possible that we may be mistaken.'

N

But while it seems to me that a church ought to require that its *Ministers* teach and practise its convictions on these subjects, ought it to require that every one of its *members* should accept them?[1] Ought it to exclude from membership every one who sincerely believes that our Lord did not institute the Eucharist as a perpetual Sacrament of His Church, and, in consequence, declines to keep this Sacrament? And, if it be said that a church ought at least to exclude those who believe in the Eucharist but neglect it, what is neglect? Will it suffice to take this Sacrament once a year? Or how often? There is probably no church in Christendom that has not been vexed with these questions, and there is perhaps none that has found a completely satisfactory answer to them. To take an historical example, it will probably be allowed by all that George Fox was a better Christian than His Majesty Charles II, yet it was the latter who took the Sacrament[2] and not the former. It may be said that Charles ought to have been turned from the table as ' an open and notorious evil liver,' but, even so, is there any test for discovering secret hypocrites and respectable formalists? Yet these too partake of the table of the Lord unworthily. In almost all churches attendance at the Lord's Supper has been made, at least nominally, a *test of membership*. I have said that I believe that our Lord Himself instituted it as a *symbol* and *means of fellowship*. Is there any difference between the two phrases? Is there a difference of value? I think there is. For it seems to me that nothing symbolic, not even the Eucharist, can by itself be an adequate *test*, and that, while many agree with this, they do not always go on to draw the right conclusion.

[1] The distinction made both here and in the preceding section, between what ought to be required of Ministers and members respectively, may not be logically defensible, but logic is not the only guide of life, nor always the best guide.

[2] e.g. *Pepys' Diary*, April 15, 1666.

To see what this is, it may be well to turn again to Wesley's ' Rules for the Societies.'   As I have already said, I believe that, while he was thinking of ' Societies,' he was in reality founding a church, and founding it in the right way.   He says, in a famous phrase, that ' there is but one condition previously required in those who desire admission into the [Methodist] Societies, viz. " *a desire to flee from the wrath to come, to be saved from their sins.*" '   These are terms of the eighteenth century.   Let us reverse the order of the clauses and use instead the terminology of to-day.   If this be done, the phrase would read, ' A desire to be saved from sin, to live now and for ever in fellowship with God through Christ.'   So stated, it is plain that we have here an account of that spiritual experience that we have already found to be central and architectonic in Christianity.   I cannot but think that the phrase is the New Testament definition of a Christian. I need perhaps to draw special attention to the first two words, ' A desire.'   Wesley held, with St. Paul and all thoroughgoing Evangelicals, that there may be more than ' desire '—that a man may enjoy conscious fellowship with Christ—and that, until he does so, he is quite an incomplete Christian.   Here falls the doctrine that the Methodist calls ' assurance.'   But, while Wesley held that this glad experience is open to all, he did not demand that every one who was admitted to his Societies should already enjoy it.   He was content to ask that they should desire it.   And this is surely enough for admission to the Church. Wesley's own mother, Susanna Wesley, did not enjoy such ' assurance ' until she was seventy years of age ; was she therefore no Christian till that age ?   Through all the conscious years of her life there had been the ' desire ' to ' know God and Jesus Christ whom He has sent.'   This suffices for Christ, and it should suffice for the Church.   For, in a sense, he who seeks God has already found Him.   God never refuses to give Himself to one

who sincerely seeks Him. The first ' thing needful ' in
a member of the Christian Church is a desire to be saved
from sin and to ' know God, and Jesus Christ, whom He
has sent.'

This experience, however, is primarily an inward thing.
Some, as we have seen, who do not exactly define the
phrase, would call it ' merely subjective.' And it is indeed
not enough that a man should just say that he wants to
know God in Christ. For he may be telling a lie. Or
he may only ' desire ' in a vague, inconstant, and otiose
way. If his desire is real and effective, it will show itself
outwardly. ' By their fruits ye shall know them.'
Wesley, therefore, goes on to say that every member of
his Societies must ' evidence [his] desire for salvation '
in two outward ways—by ' doing no harm,' and ' by
doing good . . . of every possible sort, and, as far as is
possible, to all men.' Under both these phrases he gives
a number of examples. Some of these were more pertinent in the eighteenth century than now, and the lists
make no pretence to completeness, but the point to notice
is that, having stipulated that every member should
confess his desire to know God in Christ, Wesley goes on
to demand that this shall show itself in the distinctively
Christian kind of life. From the spiritual he passes to
the ethical and moral. He adds conduct to conscience.
And he treats it as the ' fruit,' the inevitable outcome,
of the spiritual. In other words, as said above, he
requires in members of his Societies that they should
add the second and derivative essential of Christianity
to the first and primary—the moral to the spiritual. Here,
too, the sequence seems to me to be true to the New
Testament. No man is accepted by Christ—and so no
man ought to continue in the Church—who does not
desire the fellowship of Christ, and whose desire does not
manifest itself in some degree of holy life.

I need not here spend many words upon the practical

question, ' Who is to decide whether a member lives such
a life ? '   The Methodist Church throws the responsibility
initially upon two men—the Minister of the church in
which the man is a member, and a trusted layman or
laywoman, called a ' leader,' who knows the member
intimately.   If their decision is disputed, there are courts
of appeal, in which both laity and Ministers have a part.
I do not pretend that this method is perfect, but I do not
know a better.   As all Methodists know, there is a scrutiny
of the list of members four times a year, by the two
officers of the church named above.   It seems to me that,
if the above be taken as the true tests of membership, the
method justifies itself.   Few are retained in membership
who ought to be excluded ; fewer still—or rather, almost
none at all—are excluded from membership who ought
to be retained.   The chief fault is rather that not a few
who ought to be members neglect to add their names to
the list.

We come now to the third and last of our series
of elements in Christianity—the ritual and symbolic.
Wesley, of course, expected that the members of his
Societies should attend the weekly meeting of the
' Classes ' into which they were divided.   He says this
elsewhere in his Rules.   Indeed, not to attend Class was
ipso facto to cease to belong to the Society.   It seems to
me that, as Methodism ceased to be a society and became
a church, this requirement ought to have lapsed.   This
is not because I think lightly of the Class Meeting.   On
the contrary, I know few ' means of grace ' to compare
with it, when rightly used, for the deepening of the
Christian life.   It is a great organ of fellowship, and the
fellowship of Christians with Christ and with each other
is the very breath of the spiritual life of Christian men.
But, while the Class Meeting is a great means of grace,
a superb method of fellowship, it is not the only means or
the only method.   It may seem to Methodists strange to

call it a part of ritual, but, in the broad sense in which
that word is used in this Lecture, this is a true description
of it. For by ritual I mean the outward means of
fellowship. While, therefore, Wesley was right in
requiring that every member of his *Societies* should attend
the Class Meeting, the Methodist Church would not be
right in requiring that every member of that *church* should
attend. This would be to make a particular outward
ordinance essential to the Church, and, as I have already
frequently stated, this seems to me to be unjustifiable.
It is, indeed, the very error of the Sacerdotalist. The
witness of Methodism to the place of fellowship in the
Christian life is still needed ; she will do ill if she abandons
those distinctive means of fellowship that she calls
Classes ; but to attend one of these is not a necessary
qualification in a Christian man. So it should not be
requisite for membership in the Church. To make it so
results in formalism for some, a sense of the unreality
of membership for many, and the refusal of others to
become members of the Church at all.

Yet it does not follow that there is no place for ritual and
symbol in the answer to the question, ' What shall
constitute membership of the Church ? ' Let us return to
Wesley's Rules. He goes on to say that ' It is expected of
all who desire to continue in these Societies that they
should continue to evidence their desire of salvation . . .
by attending upon all the Ordinances of God ; such are—
the Public Worship of God ; the Ministry of the Word,
either read or expounded ; the Supper of the Lord ;
Family and Private Prayer ; Searching the Scriptures ;
and Fasting or Abstinence.' This list is remarkable, not
so much for the omission of Baptism—an omission that I
have already explained—as for the place given to the
Lord's Supper. I will not stay, however, to ask whether
it was set third, and not first, for any considered reason.
It seems to me that Wesley is here giving symbols their

right place in the Church. Yet there is one word in the quotation which I should change. I doubt whether a member ought to be excluded from a church because he does not attend ' *all* the Ordinances of God.' For the purposes of this Lecture it is necessary to narrow the issue yet more. These Ordinances are not all ritual or symbol. Without prayer any Christian will die. So far as I can see, since the days of the Apostles there never has been a Christian, nor ever can be, whose knowledge of Christ does not depend, directly or indirectly, upon the Bible. What are the ritual and symbolic things in the list? There is Public Worship, the Lord's Supper, and Family Prayer. All allow that a bed-ridden Christian, who cannot attend the first, ought not to be excluded from the Church. Similarly, all allow that a Christian who lives in a house where, whether he wish it or not, there is no Family Prayer, ought not to be excluded from the Church. I have argued the instance of the Lord's Supper above. Under the head of the symbolic the Wesleyan Church has tacitly made a change in its Rules, and, as I think, made the right change. Indeed, in its latest statement about membership the change is not really tacit. It excludes any who do not use *any* of the outward and ritual means of grace. This is in accordance with the findings in the second and third chapters above. There it was argued that, while no particular kind of symbol or ritual is essential to Christianity, yet the Church and the individual Christian, like all other societies and individuals, cannot but express their spiritual experience through *some* ritual and symbol. This links with another need. Every member of the Church is a member of some local church. Of which? Of the one, surely, in whose worship and Christian service he joins. It seems to me, therefore, that there is a third thing requisite in a member of the Church of Christ— that he should show by some ritual or symbol that he belongs to a particular local church, and through it to the

Church Universal. Some ritual, some symbol he must use, for he too is a man. But he need not use any particular ritual, nor any particular symbol. We reach, therefore, the old series—for membership in the Church the first requisite is membership in Christ—that is, there must at least be the desire to ' know God ' in Him ; second, it is also essential, though derivative, that a member should show this desire in the distinctive kind of Christian life ; thirdly, he must join in some effective way in the outward and symbolic and united worship of the local church to which he claims to belong. The Church ought not to confine him to any one way, not even to the way of the Lord's Supper, but it ought not to be content that a member should ignore the symbolic altogether. For, as so often asserted, it is through the symbolic that all societies live. A man might conceivably belong to a home without ever speaking ; indeed, the dumb do so sometimes ; but no man can belong to a home without communicating with the other members of it through any outward medium at all ! Similarly, a man may belong to a church even though he does not attend public worship, or a Fellowship Meeting, or even the Eucharist—but he cannot be a member of a church if he use no outward means of fellowship at all. In the Methodist Church, when a minister and ' leader ' consult whether a given member has ceased to be a member, one of the questions that they rightly ask is, ' Does he now use any of the outward means of grace ? ' I have no doubt that a similar question is asked in similar circumstances in other churches. We find, therefore, that the answer to the question, ' Who shall continue to be counted a member of the Church ? ' runs as follows : ' If he still confess his desire to know God in Christ, and if this desire manifest itself in two ways—in the ethics of a Christian life, and in the use of some outward and visible means of fellowship and grace.' It is necessary that all three be there, and as necessary that they all be there in the right order and relation to each other.

It may seem that in the last paragraphs I have forgotten that I recognize a unique obligation in the Eucharist. Here, however, I am discussing the essential, not the obligatory. Among those who hold that the Eucharist finds its proper place under the latter term there is almost a unanimous opinion that it is pre-eminently the right symbol to use as token of membership. In Evangelical churches the Eucharist is either the one symbol, or an obligatory symbol, of continuance in membership. Yet, at least in practice, they admit that there may be exceptions. Is there indeed any church, Sacramental or Sacerdotal, that excludes every one who neglects the Eucharist ?

D. Inter-Communion and Reunion

It remains to ask how Sacramental churches ought to treat other churches. What is the bearing of their opinion about ritual, symbol, and Sacrament upon questions of Inter-Communion and Reunion ? It is not possible to discuss this question without introducing another : How ought churches who do not share the Evangelical opinion about ritual and Sacrament to treat the churches that hold those opinions ? But this latter question is only considered incidentally and incompletely. It belongs to churches that repudiate the opinions here advocated, themselves to state fully how they think that they ought to treat their fellow Christians. The enemy of an opinion can hardly do justice to its practical issues. The pertinent subject here is the former question : How shall Sacramental churches treat other churches ? So far as symbol and Sacrament are concerned, the answer depends upon the opinions held about these in other churches. As already indicated, their opinions may be classified in four groups.

There are churches where the magical or superstitious opinion is operative. At least, so many Evangelical Christians think. As already seen,[1] I do not mean that there are churches where the magical opinion is *advocated*, but that there seem to me to be churches where it is *operative*. I suppose that the magical opinion has never been advocated in the Christian Church, not even in the tenth or fifteenth centuries. It has never, that is, been the authoritative teaching of any Christian church that of the three elements in the Christian religion—the spiritual, the moral, and the ritual—the last is the most important, because it inevitably carries the other two with it, or makes the other two superfluous. In theory the most extreme of Sacerdotalist churches has held that the spiritual is nobler than the ritual, and that, however necessary or essential the ritual may be, it is still of less worth than the spiritual—indeed, that without the spiritual the ritual is worthless. Romanist writers, for example, holding the doctrine of Transubstantiation itself—which is the *Ultima Thule* of the Sacerdotalist opinion—have always added, in theory, that even to ' eat ' the real ' flesh ' and to ' drink ' the real ' blood ' of God Incarnate does no good to a man who is altogether set on evil in his heart. In other words, they have taught that without at least ' a desire '—to quote Wesley's phrase—for spiritual benefit there is no benefit. But historically, theory and practice at this point fall far asunder. It is the experience of many centuries that, where the ritual and outward is made essential, it first claims equality with the spiritual, then establishes primacy over it, and finally may supersede it altogether. I do not mean, of course, that where the Sacerdotalist

[1] p. 45.

opinion prevails there are no real Christians.   To suggest
this is as monstrous as it would be untrue.   What I
mean is that hitherto in Christian history, wherever the
Sacerdotalist opinion has prevailed unchallenged for
some few generations among great masses of so-called
' Christians '—of masses, also, counted as members of
the Church—the practice, not of the Sacerdotal, but of
the magical opinion has prevailed.   Indeed, while the
two theories are logically separable, it still remains to
be shown that the one can be advocated without the
prevalence of the other.   The experience of mankind on
this subject is really much longer than the Christian era.
I have shown above how long was the agony of Israel
against the use of the image—not only against false gods,
but against the use of images of Jehovah Himself.   The
protagonists in the struggle were the Prophets.   The
Prophets were not theorists ; they were pragmatists.
It was, and is, quite possible to make a theoretic defence
of the use of images.   Indeed, it has been made, and is
still made, in Christendom, though in a different form.
But it is the universal experience of all races, in every
age, that, where the image is used in adoration, there—
not for all, but for multitudes—religion degenerates into
superstition.   By superstition I mean, of course, the
practice of the conception that, where there is the right
ritual, there is religion, whether the spiritual and the
ethical go with the ritual or not.[1]   The Evangelical does
not allow that the magical practice has vanished from
Christianity.   It was rampant in the fifteenth and preceding centuries.   While the Counter-Reformation checked
its empire in Romanist Europe, especially in the lands
where Romanism was fronted by Protestantism, to check
is not to destroy ; in many Romanist countries superstition

[1] ' It was easier to pay adoration to a picture, to reverence a relic, or to
observe a ceremony, than to regulate one's conduct in life by the principles of
morality or the doctrines of religion ' (Finlay, *History of the Byzantine Empire*,
Book I., chap. iii., sect. 3).

seems to the Evangelical to prevail to-day. What is his duty to those countries?

The Methodist Church has long sent missionaries to Romanist lands. Is this right? Or is it to be stigmatized by the ugly name ' proselytism '? The Romanist sends emissaries to Protestant countries, it is true, but, if an example be bad, there is no need to copy it. Is there good reason for seeking to spread the Evangelical faith in Romanist lands? It seems to me that the answer is: Wherever the magical concept is operative there is good reason, for the magical concept is nothing less than the reintroduction of heathenism under Christian terminology. This answer is, of course, anathema to the Sacerdotalist. But does he deny that the magical opinion prevails? If so, the question is one of fact, and it does not fall for discussion here, though there does not seem to me any real doubt what the facts are.[1] For the Evangelical there is no option. He must seek to rid Christianity of this curse. I do not mean that he need seek to destroy the ancient Sacerdotalist churches ; he need only seek to rescue them. We do indeed form Methodist churches in Italy, for instance. Yet this is admittedly an ' interim policy.' The ultimate aim is to awake in the Roman Church herself an ' Evangelical Revival.' Hitherto we have only feebly made the attempt, and we cannot complain if our critics wax a little satiric over our small success. But the endeavour is a right one. Between the magical and the Sacramental or Evangelical opinions there can be no truce.

Secondly, how shall the Sacramental churches treat Sacerdotal churches? In our own land to-day, and perhaps in other lands and times where the Sacramental opinion continually challenges the Sacerdotal, there are many Sacerdotalists who practise the Sacerdotalist creed

[1] Here Mr. Powell Williams, for instance, seems to agree (*Essays, Catholic and Critical*, pp. 394 f.).

without lapsing into magical practice. Could an Evangelical church unite with these ?

So long as the two opinions both obtain, union is only possible on one ground. In a united Church both opinions must be tolerated. For some centuries this experiment has been tried in the Anglican Church. In it there have been both Sacerdotal and Sacramental schools. Once and again, since the sixteenth century, that church has invited the Evangelical churches of England to unite with them on this basis. In effect, this was the suggestion of the famous and noble ' Appeal to all Christian People,' issued by the Lambeth Conference of Anglican bishops in 1920. In that document the bishops held out a hand each way—to the Greek and Roman churches and to the Evangelical. With the latter negotiations continued, in the way of exploration and a common attempt to find common ground, for several years. These explorations were both justifiable and desirable. They may yet bear generous fruit. But the immediate attempt at union failed upon this question, ' In a united Church, shall the ministers of Evangelical churches submit to Ordination at the hands of bishops who are in what is called " the Apostolical Succession " ? ' It is plain that a Sacerdotalist could not consent to admit their ' orders ' without this. To do so would be to contradict his whole theory. Some think that it is not so clear why the Evangelical churches should refuse Episcopal Ordination. It is said, ' While you submit to this rite, you can still hold the Sacramental opinion. You can submit to Episcopal Ordination even though you think that it adds nothing to your ministry. In the Anglican Church there are already many who hold your opinion about it ; you will only add to their numbers.' This is honest reasoning,[1] but, if there be truth in the argument of this Lecture, it is

---

[1] Yet I am not sure that those who urge it have always put themselves in the place of men who are asked to leave the validity of their Ordination an open question.

plain, I think, that the Free Church representatives were right in their reluctant refusal. There are indeed questions about which two opinions may be tolerated in the Church of Christ, but this does not seem to me to be one of them. The choice is like the choice between ' two diphthongs ' at the Council of Constantinople. The followers of Athanasius were right in the contention that the real choice was between a belief in the divinity of our Lord and its rejection. So here, while the choice seems to resolve into a mere matter of one ceremony more or less, the real decision is between a spiritual and a materialist conception of the Church of Christ. For to admit that any particular outward symbol is essential to the Church is to begin to materialize it. We cannot even tolerate the opinion that God the Holy Spirit is limited in a way that seems to us untrue. The history of the Church from the days of Cyprian to those of Luther is loud with the consequences of that error. Our opponents, of course, reject such a judgement of history. But do they not agree that for us, who cannot but pass this judgement, only one course is open ?

Perhaps here again I may turn aside for a moment to say a word to ' practical men.' Some of them say, ' Get this little theoretical question of Ordination out of the way, and get on with your true work as a united Church.' If any such ' practical man ' has read this Lecture so far, he will see the answer. It is only in appearance that the issue is small. Not infrequently a great issue concentrates upon a seemingly small point. It might be said that the struggle between Crown and Parliament in the days of the Stuarts was about the paltry question whether inland counties, as well as maritime, should help to pay for the king's ships. Or one might say that the dispute between England and her American Colonies in the eighteenth century was just over the payment of a small tax on tea. Or one might say that Paul strove with the

' Judaizers ' about the use of the unimportant ceremony
of circumcision. Or it might be said that Luther and
Leo quarrelled over the theoretical relation of faith and
works in the Christian life, and that this doesn't matter
much so long as both are there. But historians know that
these seeming trifles are only the tokens of great and
far-reaching differences. It is the same with the question
of Episcopal Ordination. In itself it is no bigger than
the question whether this face or that shall be stamped on
a coin. Yet many a wise monarch has been very resolute
about the right of coinage. Or to use another figure, the
turn of a rudder decides the way of a ship. If the long
history of Christian superstition be once more recalled,
and it be recalled also that, where the Sacerdotal opinion
has reigned, superstition has always ensued, perhaps
' practical men ' will allow that it is right to treat the
question of Episcopal Ordination as index of a great and
far-reaching issue.

If the Sacramentalist and the Sacerdotalist cannot
unite, can they practise Inter-Communion ? Before this
question can be answered, it is necessary to ask another :
What is Inter-Communion ?

As soon as the word is examined, it is found to cover
several separate questions. For instance, are two
churches in Inter-Communion if they recognize the
validity of each other's Baptisms ? Or must they also
admit that the Eucharist as administered in each church
is a true Eucharist ? Or must they also allow that both
churches have a true Ministry ? Must they allow that
the Ministers of the one church may properly take part
in all the services of the other ? In Ordination ? In
administering the two Sacraments ? In preaching ?
And so on. Perhaps for the present purpose the best
account of Inter-Communion is this : Two churches are
in Inter-Communion when they admit each other's
members to the Eucharist without demur, when they allow

each other's Ministers to adminster the Sacrament of
the Lord's Supper in each other's churches, when they
recognize the validity of each other's Ordinations, and
when they raise no objection, at least in theory, to
Ministers of the one church taking part in the Ordination
of Ministers in the other. This is the account of Inter-
Communion that governs the discussion of this subject
in the Lambeth Report of 1920. Under it, for instance,
the Anglican Church expresses its willingness to hold
Inter-Communion with the Church of Sweden. On the
other hand, the Lambeth Report makes no such offer
to the Free Churches of England. The most that it
offers to them is an occasional and carefully-guarded
' interchange of pulpits,' the recognition of the validity
of their Baptisms, and the regulation that, when any one
presents himself for the reception of the Elements in the
Eucharist, an Anglican celebrant shall not pause to
inquire whether he has been ' confirmed ' or not. I do
not wish to depreciate the value or generosity of these
directions, for I think that in the Lambeth Report the
Anglican bishops went as far in their friendly offers of
something like Inter-Communion to the English Free
Churches as they consistently could. If anything, they
' strained a point ' on the side of generosity. I am one
of a great multitude of Free Churchmen who rejoice
unfeignedly in the warmth and depth of their charity.
The pertinent point here is a comparatively small one—
to show that, according to the definition of Inter-
Communion that the bishops, as it seems to me, rightly
adopted, they found themselves able to offer to practise
it with the Swedish Church but not with the Free Churches
of England.

With this definition of Inter-Communion, it follows that
it is easier for a Sacramentalist to offer it to a Sacerdotalist
church than vice versa. For the Sacramentalist does not
doubt the validity of the Sacraments and Ordinations in

a Sacerdotalist church, while the latter denies the validity of these in a Sacramentalist church. It follows, for instance, that a Sacerdotalist can neither invite Free Churches to take part in the Eucharist in his own church, nor accept invitations to share with them in the administration in their churches. The objection to Inter-Communion, in other words, lies with him and not with them. His principles do not allow him to follow as ' catholic ' a practice—to use the word in its true sense— as their principles allow them. This one fact does not certainly mean that he is wrong. Some Unitarian Ministers hold such ' broad ' opinions that they could join in administering a Sacrament in any church ; a true Sacramentalist must decline their help ; it follows that, in the literal sense, these Unitarians are more ' catholic ' than Sacramentalists ; but it would not follow that the Unitarians are right. But the practical result of the differences between the Sacerdotalist and Sacramentalist is this—while the latter is able, at least theoretically, to offer to practise Inter-Communion with the former, the former cannot practise it with the latter. On the definition given, therefore, there cannot be Inter-Communion.

It follows, too, that the bishops were right in carefully guarding ' interchange of pulpits.' If such interchange were frequent, and if there were no conditions, it might soon happen that a Sacramentalist, preaching in an Anglican church, might, at least by inadvertent implication, repudiate the Sacerdotalist opinion that the Anglican Church tolerates. Similarly, a Sacerdotalist, preaching in one of the Free churches, might, through the mere trend of his customary thought, imply the doctrine that he loves. In either instance there might ensue just that kind of contention that all sincere Christians count a scandal. The practical rule seems to follow that, while the Sacramentalist will delight to accept all opportunities

O

of showing that among all Christians there is much truth held in common, he will be careful lest the very zeal of his charity should lead him astray. Here the bishops, guiding a church that has both Sacramentalists and Sacerdotalists within it, showed us all how to blend wisdom, courage, and charity.

Can a Sacramentalist church unite with those who repudiate all symbols, like the first Quakers, or even with those, like many of the Quakers of to-day, who recognize that it is impossible to do without symbols, but seek to use them as little as possible ? The question answers itself. The Sacramentalist believes that the two Sacraments were ordained by Christ Himself ; and, apart from this, he believes that the outward and symbolic has a true, though a secondary, place in worship, and he seeks to use it as far as it is serviceable. There is an old question, ' How can two walk together except they be agreed ? ' Here it resolves into another : ' How can two walk together when they are going in opposite directions ? ' A Sacramentalist, however, and a Quaker may each cherish his own hope. The Quaker may hope that the Sacramentalist, having repudiated the doctrine that particular symbols are essential to Christianity, will go on to do his best to discard them altogether. The Sacramentalist, on the other hand, may hope that the Quaker, having discovered that to do without symbol wholly is impossible, may be content to join with those who assert that it is non-essential. This, indeed, was the real claim of the first Friends. There is no need to say which hope I myself cherish. [1]

Can a Sacramentalist meanwhile practise Inter-Communion with the Friends ? The answer is of the same

[1] Perhaps the Salvation Army should be named here, for, though Salvationists have a symbolism of their own, they do not observe either Sacrament. I am among those who hope that, as they grow into a church, they will come to do so. At present Christian thought pays far too little attention to the great phenomenon of the Salvation Army. But, then, it is only just beginning to take serious account of that earlier phenomenon, Methodism.

kind as when the question is asked of the Sacerdotalist. While the Sacramentalist would not refuse the Sacraments to a Friend, the Friend cannot ask for them so long as he holds extreme Quaker principles. It is the Friend rather than the Sacramentalist whose conscience requires him to refuse Inter-Communion. The Sacramentalist and Friend will welcome all opportunities even of a partial Inter-Communion, though here again they will use them with Christian wariness. In particular, a Sacramentalist addressing a Friends' meeting, or a Friend speaking to a Sacramentalist church, will need to watch his thoughts as well as his lips, lest, even unawares, he implicitly advocate the opinions that his hearers reject. To practise a limited Inter-Communion needs more than a hearty goodwill, though that carries Christians far. This practice is as difficult as some others in the fine art of love.

The fourth opinion about symbols has throughout been called Sacramental. It is held, not only by Methodists, but by other Evangelical churches—by the Presbyterian churches, for example, and the Congregational and the Baptist. Can these churches seek to unite with each other ? Can they practise a full Inter-Communion ?

The answer to the second question is, ' They already do so, at least in theory, and largely in practice.' [1] If a member of one church wishes to join another, he is accepted without demur ; a Minister may pass from one to another without Re-ordination ; all accept the validity of the Sacraments as administered in all ; there is no reason why the Ministers of one of them should not join in the Ordination of the Ministers of another. So far as I know, there is as yet no instance of this being done. For

[1] Two exceptions may be named—first, the Baptists have, of course, distinctive convictions about the Sacrament of Baptism ; this has been referred to above. Second, the Church of Scotland, some twenty-five years ago, re-ordained a Wesleyan Minister who sought admission to that church ; whether the Church of Scotland would do so to-day I do not know.

myself, I wish that it might now be done, for this would be a kind of final witness to the completeness of Inter-Communion between the Evangelical churches.

Can the Sacramental churches seek union with each other? The answer is that, so far as the subject of this Lecture goes, there is nothing to hinder. And, as it seems to me, where there is no objection on the ground of principle, there a sincere Christian will earnestly seek to reunite the sundered Church of Christ. The Sacramental churches differ in other ways, notably about Church government. It does not appear to-day that any of these differences are differences of principle, though they may have seemed so in the past. And surely the right place to undertake sedulously and unfalteringly the task of reuniting the Church of Christ is where the differences are not differences of principle, but only of method. To admit, as I have admitted more than once above, that at present there seems to be no way to bridge the gulf between the Sacramentalist and the Sacerdotalist, happily does not commit either to abandon the enterprise of reunion. It only limits for both the sphere of that enterprise. Is not the sphere that is left to Evangelicals wide enough for our present endeavours? By the time we have achieved the task that immediately awaits us, God may have made manifest the way to undertake the wider one. Sometimes He shows clearly a nearer height to His mountaineers, while yet the utmost summit is hid in cloud.

APPENDIX

SOME POSTULATES

THERE are three postulates in the above discussion, about which something has been said incidentally, but which it does not belong to the purpose of this Lecture fully to examine. Perhaps I ought to add a summary statement about each.

1. THE POSTULATE OF ANALOGY

Science has a postulate called 'the uniformity of nature.' 'The unity of nature' is perhaps a better name, for science holds, not that nature repeats itself, but that there is harmony, or congruity, or system, in nature. It is admitted to-day that there is also endless variety and novelty, but the postulate of uniformity has not therefore been abandoned. Every man of science takes it for granted that every new phenomenon forms part of a great system. Some would even say that every phenomenon, whether new or old, is what it is because the whole of the rest of nature is what it is. This is to carry the notion of system to its utmost limit. Many think that there never can be any proof of this scientific postulate, yet every investigation of phenomena confirms the faith of those who accept it. It is the universal assumption of science.

So long as miracle was defined as an interruption of the order of nature, there was sure to be strife between religion and science, for the one denied the other's most cherished postulate. It claimed that there were a certain number of events that did not harmonize with the rest of the system of nature—that contradicted its uniformity. This battle no longer rages. And it no longer rages because the Christian apologist has so restated his creed that he accepts the doctrine of the uniformity of nature, and defines miracle in a new way.

The Christian's equivalent for the uniformity of nature is the immanence of God. Or rather, the doctrine of immanence includes all that the scientific phrase means. If we leave out sin, the Christian claims that God is at work in all nature—that He is its great artist—and that its system is due to His operative mind. It is indeed harmonious, or a system : its parts are indeed congruous with each other : for it is His ' workmanship,' His poem.

This concept of immanence carries with it a new definition of miracle. Under the old definition God was thought of as usually leaving the universe alone, but now and then interfering by the intrusion of the so-called supernatural. But under the new concept of God the natural and the super-natural coincide. God is in everything : He is not to be isolated to a few events. In other words, everything is miracle, if by miracle is meant the action of God. If the word is to be kept for a few events, the only meaning that can now be attached to it is to make it mean an event that displays the divine action with unusual clearness. In other words, the definition of miracle is relative to human knowledge. In earlier days men cried out ' miracle ! ' when they saw a comet, but they took the sun for granted. To-day we know that God's power is just as clearly evident in the one as the other. Or again, God was at work in all that Christ did. In Jesus the Father spoke to men through both the usual and the unusual. But men saw God's work more readily in the extraordinary works of Christ than in the ordinary. And the former were called miracles. To-day we are more prone to see God in the everyday life of Jesus. Miracle is not now a name for a few events in which alone God is at work among men, but for a few events among the multitudinous works of an immanent God that specially strike the attention of men.

It follows from this account of immanence and of miracle that there are no exceptions in God's universe. The men of science have a right to their postulate. All phenomena must fall into harmony. There is congruity and system in all the works of God. Jesus' miracles, for instance, are in harmony with the belief that He was the Incarnate Son. This being so, there is a valid use of analogy in theology. From one part of God's poem we can learn something about another part. This does not mean that all the parts are alike, for the theologian, like the man of science, admits and exults in the variety and novelty of the universe. But it does mean that there is congruity and harmony amid the variety. It does mean, for instance, that God is not likely to pursue one use of symbol in the Sacraments and another in the rest of human life. It does mean that even among the mysteries of the Christian faith there is consistency. This belief or postulate lies behind the whole of the discussion above. It seems to me to be a thoroughly scientific postulate. On the other hand, the Sacerdotalist, when he asserts that in Ordination or Baptism or the Eucharist there is a ' miracle,' seems to me to be working with the old and exploded definition. He postulates something that is incongruous with the rest of God's universe. He pleads for the exceptional in the sense of the contradictory. As I have tried to show above, this seems peculiarly clear when the word ' miracle ' is used of a supposed change in the elements at the Eucharist—a change of which no man ever had or can have evidence. But the error, for so I must needs think it, is involved in the whole Sacerdotal theory. The theory of the Apostolical Succession, for instance, or the doctrine of Baptismal Regeneration, as well as the doctrine of the Physical Presence in the Eucharist, are out of joint with the universe. Elsewhere God does not act so. On the other hand, the Sacramental account of Ordination and Baptism and the Eucharist, as well as of all other Christian symbols, seems to me, as I have tried to show above, to be in harmony with the rest of the ways of God.

2. OUR LORD'S RELATION TO THE TWO SACRAMENTS

As already stated, I am among those who believe that our Lord Himself instituted the two Sacraments, and meant them to be perpetual among His followers. If any one objects to the term ' institute,' when applied to Baptism, on the ground that a similar rite was in use among the Jews for the reception of Gentiles into Judaism, and that John the Baptist had used it before Jesus, I am content to yield him the verbal point and to substitute ' enjoin ' for ' institute.' It is admitted by all that the Sacrament of Baptism was practised by the Church from the Day of Pentecost onwards. Why ? It is true that the so-called Formula of Baptism at the end of the First Gospel may not be phrased in the *ipsissima verba* of Jesus. But the existence of the Formula in the *Jewish* Christian Church for which our First Gospel was written, by about A.D. 80, and the universal acceptance in that Church, of this account of the origin of Christian Baptism, seem to me decisive proof that our Lord taught His disciples to baptize, and instructed them to continue to use the rite. It is one thing to say that the *ipsissima verba* of the passage named are not His, another to say that the tradition that they convey is false. If it is false, why was Baptism universal in the Church from the first ? Was it a sudden idea of Peter's at Pentecost ? The evidence of the Fourth Gospel, again, is far from negligible.[1] There seems to me to be good evidence that our Lord taught His disciples to baptize, and intended that the practice should continue after His death.

No one denies that there was a Last Supper. The evidence that our Lord meant the Eucharist to be perpetual among His disciples seems to me very good. It is true that the words, ' This do in remembrance of Me,' only occur certainly in St. Paul's account of the institution, but no one doubts that the rite had been observed from the very first days of the Church. Why? Does any one think that Paul invented this reason? Surely He is only expressing what all believed. And, so far as I can see, if our Lord did not intend the Supper to be repeated, it is difficult, or even impossible, to give any reasonable account of what He said at the table. There is no difficulty, of course, in supposing that ' with desire ' He should ' desire ' to gather with His dear ones once more at the familiar board before He ' suffered.' But why should He say, ' This is My body,' and ' This is My blood of the covenant ' ? It seems to me that there is here a far more serious difficulty than St. Mark's omission of the words, ' This do in remembrance of Me.' In the Church for which he wrote this would be just one of those obvious things that everybody takes for granted. Again, no one suggests that Mark tells us everything that Jesus said in the Upper Room.

Reference should be made to the argument that Jesus would not appoint rites of perpetual obligation because, under the eschatological creed of His time, He expected soon to return to inaugurate the Kingdom of God. It seems to me that, while He said that He did not know certainly when the Kingdom would come,[2] He did expect it soon.[3] ' Soon,' however, is not the same as ' immediately.' Jesus Himself repudiated the opinion that the Kingdom should ' immediately appear.'[4] He expected an interval, though not a long interval, before the Parousia, and there seems no good reason for asserting that He would not provide His disciples with distinctive Sacraments of union during the interval. He founded a society, whether He called it ' church ' or not, and the two Sacraments were among its marks.

3. THE MYSTERY RELIGIONS AND THE NEW TESTAMENT

It has appeared above that I agree with those who think that some recent writers have greatly exaggerated the influence of the Mystery Religions upon the Apostolic Church. Broadly speaking,

[1] John iii. 24, iv. 1 f.   [2] Matt. xxiv. 36.   [3] Matt. xxiv. 34.
[4] Luke xix. 11 ; cf. Matt. xxiv. 6, 14.

the experts on this subject fall into two schools. One school holds that, while the Christian writers of the New Testament, and in particular St. Paul and St. John, occasionally use phraseology current in these religions, the distinctively Christian belief about the two Sacraments was not of the same type as that of the devotees of the Mystery Religions about their 'Sacraments.' The other school holds that the Pauline doctrine of the Sacraments is nothing more than a variant of the doctrine of the Mystery Religions—that by Baptism and the Eucharist as mere rites—or *ex opere operato*—a Christian was 'born again' and assured of immortality. It seems to me that the first school are right, though I can only give the reasons very summarily. It is agreed that the cult of the Mystery Religions was rife in the Gentile world of the first century, but it is also agreed that the cult was secret. Writers of the second school declare that some customs of these secret cults were known to all—so well known, indeed, that St. Paul, for instance, writing to the Corinthian church, could take it for granted that every member of the Church would be familiar with them. Now it is possible that every one may know some things about a prevalent secret ritual. For instance, it is perhaps true that every one to-day knows some things about the ritual of the Freemasons, though it might be difficult exactly to give a list of these things. But the things generally known about secret cults are things that are common among them. Now, it seems certain that no customs really parallel to the Christian Eucharist were *usual* in the Mystery Cults. At most, some rather similar observances may be discerned in one or two of them.[1] There is no proof at all, for instance, that it was *customary* in them to observe a ritual of eating a god. We need proof that a custom like the Eucharist was so general in the secret Mystery Cults that 'everybody' would know of it, and we are offered some obscure and doubtful parallels in one or two of them! As to Baptism, lustration is so natural a symbol of cleansing that it is not surprising to find it, in one form or another, in many cults, but there is no proof that its Christian form was particularly like that of the Mystery Religions. Again, it is to be remembered that the characteristic words in the ritual of both the Christian Sacraments passed to the Gentile churches from the Jewish, and that it is very unlikely indeed that the Mystery Cults influenced Palestinian Jews. Was it not the glory of Israel

---

[1] See, for instance—to quote writers of different schools—H. A. A. Kennedy, *St. Paul and the Mystery Religions*; Percy Gardner, 'The Pagan Mysteries' (in *The Modern Churchman*, October 1926), and Powell Williams in *Essays, Catholic and Critical*.

that its religion was unlike that of other people's? When John baptized, was he teaching a Mystery Cult? Again, in the history of the Eucharist the fontal phrases—' This is My body,' ' This cup is the new covenant in My blood '—go back to our Lord Himself. Was He copying the Mystery Religions? Yet it is round these phrases that Paul weaves those others that are supposed to be so decisive. Finally, was Paul himself likely to accept any doctrine from anywhere that taught that a man entered into the Kingdom of Heaven by mere ritual? In his struggle with the Judaizers he had striven to the death against the claim that any outward thing could be essential to Christianity. He had maintained that even outward morality by itself was not enough. Did such a man yield, without a murmur or even without knowing what he was doing, to the pretensions of heathen rites? Did this devoted Jew, having torn himself away from Judaism because he found that nothing outward can save the soul, and having striven almost to the point of schism against those within the Christian Church who urged that an outward rite was necessary to salvation, yield the very issue without a word to his Gentile environment? It is not too much to say that any other possible exegesis of his words is to be preferred to one that requires so great a marvel. And, as appears above, it seems to me that there is not only another possible exegesis, but a more probable one.

INDEX OF SCRIPTURE REFERENCES

THE OLD TESTAMENT

THE NEW TESTAMENT

INDEX OF NAMES AND SUBJECTS

INDEX OF NAMES AND SUBJECTS